AF531755

NEW INNOVATION IN BANKING SECTOR

NEW INNOVATION IN BANKING SECTOR

Edited by

Dr. Rabi Narayan Misra

M.Com., LLB., M.Phil, Ph.D.

and

Dr. B.P.N. Reddy

Lecturer in Commerce

V.K.V. Govt. Degree College

Kothapeta E.D. (Dist.)

Andhra Pradesh

(India)

DISCOVERY PUBLISHING HOUSE PVT. LTD.

NEW DELHI-110 002

Published by:

Tilak Wasan

DISCOVERY PUBLISHING HOUSE PVT. LTD.
4383/4B, Ansari Road, Darya Ganj
New Delhi-110 002 (India)
Phone : +91-11-23279245, 43596064-65
Fax : +91-11-23253475
E-mail : discoverypublishinghouse@gmail.com
sales@discoverypublishinggroup.com
web : www.discoverypublishinggroup.com

***First Edition:* 2015**

ISBN: 978-93-5056-727-2

New Innovation in Banking Sector

Printed at:
Infinity Imaging Systems
Delhi

PREFACE

For the socio-Economic development of the country, role of banks are to be considered more vital. A remarkable change has been indicated after globalization. At present, due to development of information technology, the banking sector has become most important for day-to-day living. Innovation approach of banking sector is to increase the value of customers by introducing ATM, internet banking etc. has make the customer effective and able to meet the challenges. This book will very much helpful to research scholars, bankers as well as to the government.

Dr. R.N. Misra

Dr. B.P.N. Reddy

ACKNOWLEDGEMENTS

We are very much thankful to all paper writers of this book. We are also express our thanks to Mr. Tilak Wason, the owner of the Discovery Publishing House (P) Ltd., New Delhi for his kind co-operation and help in publishing this book in time. Further, we are also grateful to P. Wasan, the real leader of the Discovery Publishing House (P) Ltd. and his team of dedicated recourses persons for publishing this book in neat and clean.

Dr. R.N. Misra

Dr. B.P.N. Reddy

CONTENTS

1

Significant Innovations and Challenges in Banking Sectors of India

—Dr. Brajamohan Sasmal*

In the recent advancing age of Information Technology and internet system there is rapid and remarkable developmental changes in banking industries of India. Most of the banking sectors have adopted innovative approach towards banking system with the objective of creating more value for customers in the banks, in rural as well as in urban areas. Since the Independence of India, the bank industries have already undergone a huge transformation, particularly during the period 1990s to 2000s. Some of the significant innovations and challenges in banking industries in India have been discussed below:

Since 1990s, the banking sectors in India saw remarkable developmental changes as a result of greater emphasis given on advanced technology and innovative approach. Indian banks began to use advanced technology to provide better services to the customers at greater speed than past. Internet banking and mobile banking systems made it more convenient and comfortable for customers to do their banking from geographically diverse places. Bank sector also enhanced their focus on rural markets and introduced a variety of services to gear up the special needs of their customers. Banking activities also been sharpened their

*Retired Professor, Sheragada Bunglow, Brahmapur (Ganjam), Odisha, India.

traditional scopes and new attractive and time-saving concepts like personal banking, retailing, and bank assurances were introduced. The bank sectors are also moving rapidly towards universal or global banking and recent electronic transactions, which were expected to change the way banking which will be perceived in the future.

Since the year 2000, the banking sectors have undergone many changes. Most of the banks have started taking an innovative approach towards banking with the objective of creating more value of customers. Some of the significant changes in Indian banking sectors are discussed below:

Technology for Value Creation

The use of information technology in the Indian banking sectors was a corollary of the liberalization process initiated in the country in the early 1990s, in order to create more value of customers.

Banking in Rural Sectors

The rural banking forms a vital component of Indian banking system, as majority of Indian population live in rural areas. Besides, rural banking operations in India are rather different from urban operations, due to the strong disparity that exists between urban and rural life and the needs of these two sections of people.

Banking Beyond Banking

In the later parts of 20th century, the word banking took a different meaning altogether, while traditionally banking meant "borrowing and lending of money". Banks no longer restricted themselves and captured new markets.

The Changing Face of Banking

Many experts in banking management predict more revolutionary changes in the field of banking sectors in future. Among the changes the concepts of universal banking and smart card technology are most likely to be introduced very shortly. Although, the Indian banking sector has made rapid progress by introduction of innovative approaches, some analysts questioned about the efficiency and practical use of many of these services. Financial sector reforms initiated in the country as a part of the economic reforms since the year 1991, has brought a about revolution in the structure of banking environment. While deregulation has opened up new opportunities for banks, liberalisation has (intensified competition in the banking industry by opening the market to new, foreign and private sector banks. Declining interest rates and reduced lending margins have thrown up new challenges to banks, particularly public sector banks. Banks need to equip themselves sufficiently to operate in such a competitive environment. In 1996, the World Bank made commitment to become a global knowledge bank. The banks' stated intention was to develop a world class knowledge management system and to improve and expand the sharing of development knowledge with clients and partners. The main objectives of this commitment were to improve the quality of bank operations and to enhance the capacity of clients to achieve development of results.

Global Challenges in Banking

1. Enhancement of customer service
2. Innovations in technology
3. Improvement of risk management systems.
4. Diversifying products
5. **Globalisation in banking:** Challenges are not restricted only to global banks. Banks in India also need to face them. Overcoming these challenges makes them more competitive and will also equip them to launch themselves as global players.

Competitions

Globalisation has brought competition in banking sectors at par with the international banks, in order to compete with the fully developed banks, commercial banks and to possess strong balance sheets, which indicate the real strength of the bank. The entry of the new private sector banks and foreign banks equipped with latest technology have really sensitized the ordinary customers of banking services to need for quality in terms of innovative products, as well as delivery process. These banks are rapidly targeting the retail business and consequently capturing the market share of public sector banks.

Electronic Banking

In future the banking sector will be actually driven by the improved technology and telecommunication systems. Aided by newly advanced electronic technology, public sector banks have made rapid advancement in product innovation and delivery thereby improving quality of customer service. The advanced electron banking system has changed the definition of banking as "Triple A" — Banking Any time, Any where Banking and Any how banking. The internet banking enables three profit centres namely, treasury, corporate banking, retail banking to launch new products and quality service to a wider customer sector.

Technology

By the help of innovative information technology, banks are able to reduce the transaction cost and handle a large number of transactions in time. Now banks can provide customized products easily and customers could access many services through internet by sitting at home. To provide better services to their customers, banks are adopting Customer Relationship Management (CRM), facilitated by availability of conducive technology. The innovation is a technology which is also helping banks to cross sell the products of insurance and security firms, which increase their fee based income in the total income. Innovative technology not only brings better benefits, but also risks too.

Innovations in Housing Loans

Nowadays, banks are concentrating more on housing loans. The booming housing loans market positively affects many industries. So, to provide special interest to any economy, booming housing market is vital. Banks are benefited by high security, low risk weights and reasonable margins.

Risk Management

Globalisation and liberalisation are forcing banks to take more risk to compete effectively in the global market place. One of the important risks is compliance risk. It is the risk to comply with laws, rules and standards such as market conduct, treating customers fairly etc. To mitigate this risk, banks should develop compliance functions that are in consistence with compliance. The liquidity risk arises when banks unable to meet their obligations when they become due. To manage the mismatching of assets and liabilities they should analyse the accounting date on static as well as dynamic basis. Deposits of higher value are the most important items to be monitored regularly as sudden withdrawal of these deposits might cause liquidity problem for the bank. Sometimes incentives to these deposits in time falling interest rates could create strain on liquidity.

Innovations in Customer Services

Satisfied customer is the best guarantee for stability of the organisation in the long run. Banks can satisfy their customers only by providing customized, cost effective and timely services. With the help of the technology banks are able to provide enough, products and services to their customers which suit them. Major services provided by the Indian banks that are of international standards are Any time banking, Any where banking, Global ATM, Credit Cards, internet Banking etc.

Conclusion

The innovative approach in banking sector has definitely brought out a remarkable revolutionary changes in banking through advanced technologies such as electronic banking and internet banking. This approach is accomplished through more effective products* processes, services, technologies or ideas that are readily available to markets, governments and society. By innovative approaches the banking sector in India has become stronger in terms of capital and the number of customers. Now a days it has become globally competitive and diverse aiming at higher productivity and efficiency. Reforms through innovative approaches have changed the face of Indian banking and finance. Actually speaking, the banking sector has improved manifolds in terms of technology, and advanced means of innovations.

2

Service Sector Finance by SBI—A Study

—Dr. S.K. Badatya*

Introduction

Indian economy had experienced major policy changes nearly 1990s. The new economic reform, popularly known as, Liberalization, Privatization and Globalization (LPG model) aimed at making the Indian economy as fastest growing economy and globally competitive. The series of reforms undertaken respect to industrial sector, trade as well as financial sector aimed at making the economy more efficient. With the onset of reforms to liberalization the Indian economy in July of 1991, a new chapter has dawned for India and her billions plus population. This period economic transition has had a tremendous impact on the overall economic development of almost all major sectors of the economy, and its effects over the last decade can hardly be overlooked. Besides, it also marks the advent of the real integration of the Indian economy into the global economy. Now that India is in the process of restructuring her economy, with aspirations of elevating herself from her present desolate position in the world, the need to speed up her economic development is even more imperative.

The State Bank of India (SBI) which is the largest and the premier bank among the commercial banks of the country, has occupied a unique place in the Indian Money Market

*Senior Faculty Member of MBA, SMIT, Berhampur.

(IMM) as commands more than one-third of India's banking resources. SBI came into existence on 1st July 1955 after the nationalization of the Imperial Bank of India with the help of the State Bank of India Act which was passed by the Government of India on 8th May 1955. One of the basic objectives of setting up the SBI was extension of banking facility on large scale more particularly on the rural and semi-urban areas. It plays an important role in financing the priority sectors. Service Sector is the lifeline for the social economic growth of a country. It is today the largest and fastest growing sector and contributing more to the global output and provides employment to more people than any other sector.

The term 'Globalization' refers to the integration of economics of the world through uninhibited trade and financial flows as also mutual exchange of technology and knowledge. Ideally it also contains free inter-country movement of labours. In context to India this implies to opening up economy to Foreign Direct Investment (FDI) by providing facilities to foreign companies to invest in different fields of economy in India, removing constraints obstacles to entry of MNCs in India, allowing Indian companies to enter into foreign collaborations and also encouraging them to setup joint ventures abroad.

As we well known globally due to growing territory of several economics, service sector has an emerged as the largest and fast growing sector in the global economy in the past two decades. The service sector in India has been growing expontially since 90s. The FDI increased in following sectors such as power management, IT, telecom etc. These fields provided India with abundant employment and avenues for improving India's infrastructures. Due to globalizations not only the GDP has increased but also the direction of growth in the sectors has also changed. Earlier, the maximum part of the GDP in the economy was generated from the primary sector but now the services industry is devoting the maximum part of the GDP. The service sector remains the growth driver of the economy with contribution of more than 57 per cent of GDP. India is ranked 18th among the world's leading exporters of services with a share of 1.3 per cent in world exports. Thus, we find that the economic reforms in the Indian economy since July 1991 have led to fiscal consolidation, control of inflation to some extent, increase in foreign exchange reserves and greater flow of foreign investment and technology towards India. The percentage of agriculture, industry and services to GDP was 35.2 per cent, 26.1 per cent and 38.7 per cent respectively in the year 1984-85 whereas in the year 2010 the share of these three sectors is 15.80, 25.80 and 58.40 per cent respectively.

Objectives of the Study

1. To know the share of service sector to GDP during the study period.
2. To analyse the performance of SBI in financing towards service sector in Ganjam districts during the study period.
3. To analyse the recovery position of SBI towards financing service sector in sample district.

Limitations of the Study

The different banks of Ganjam district played important role in financing service sector. The SBI played a vital role in economic development of Ganjam district particularly in priority sector. For the purpose of the study we have taken 300 sample beneficiaries randomly those were financed by SBI for three sectors during the study period. Due to short span of time we have taken only 300 samples during the study period of past five years from 2000-01 to 2008-09. We collect data from the borrowers about the financing styles of SBI. As per borrower's views and opinions, we prepared the questionnaires so it has its own limitations. For evaluation of performance, the ratios, percentage have been computed by using the data available in various sources.

Structure of the Economy

Due to globalization not only the GDP has increased but also the direction of growth in the sectors has also changed. Earlier the maximum part of the GDP in the economy was generated from the primary sector but now the service sector is devoting the maximum part of the GDP. The service sector remains the growth driver of the economy with contribution of more than 57 per cent of GDP. India is ranked 8th among the world's leading exporters of services with share of 1.3 per cent in world exports. After liberalization growth of service sector is due to growth of software, ITES -BPO sectors in recent years.

Table 2.1: Structure of the Economy of India

(in percentage)

% of GDP	1984-85	2002-03	2003-04	2004-05	2005-06	2007-08	2008-09	2009-10
Agriculture	35.2	26.5	21.7	20.5	20	17	17.5	15.80
Industry	26.1	22.1	26.1	21.9	26	29	20	25.80
Services	38.7	51.4	56.7	57.6	54	54	62.5	58.40
Total	100.0	100.0	100.0	100.0	100.0	100.0	100.0	100.0

Source: *Economic Survey of India*, 2010-11.

Table 2.1 has explained that the share of both agricultural and industrial sectors to GDP decreases from 35.2 per cent to 15.80 per cent and 26.1 per cent to 25.8 per cent respectively during the period 1984-85 to 2009-10. Only the service sector increases its share to the GDP from 38.7 per cent to 58.40 per cent

during the same period. It has also been seen from the table that in the year 2008-09 the share of service sector is more than 60 per cent whereas share of both industrial and agriculture sectors-less than 40 per cent. Industrial sector also decreases it share from 26 per cent to 20 per cent during the same period. The growth of service sector after globalization is due to increase in foreign exchange reserve, greater flow of foreign investment and technology towards India, control of inflation etc. After the globalization in 1991 the condition of agriculture has not improved, it's share of GDP has decreased to 15.8 per cent from 35 per cent during the period 1984-85 to 2009-10 beneficiaries.

Analysis of the Study

The State Bank of India (SBI) of Ganjam district extends its loan facilities to not only for service sector but also for other sectors such as agriculture and industries. To know the performance of the SBI the data have been classified on the basis of sector-wise finance, recovery of finance and finance as per the requirements of the borrowers. The sector-wise finance made by SBI towards service sector is illustrated in Table 2.2.

The Sector-wise Finance made by SBI

The sector-wise loan sanction to the sample beneficiaries by the SBI is explained in Table 2.2. The 300 borrowers have been taken from eight sample districts of Southern Orissa for our study. The finance made to them by the SBI of the sample districts are explained in Table 2.2.

Table 2.2 : Sector-wise Finance made by SBI to Sample Beneficiaries of Ganjam District of Orissa

Sl. No.	Different Sectors	No. of beneficiaries	Amount Sanctioned (Rs. in crores)	Percentage
1.	Service Sector	100	2.53	51.5
2.	Agricultural Sector	100	1.26	25.6
3.	Industrial sector	100	1.12	22.9
	Total	300	4.91	100.0

Source: Compiled from questionnaires.

From Table 2.2, it is very clear that the SBI sanctioned maximum amount towards beneficiaries of service sector i.e. 2.53 crore which constitute 51.5 percent of total fund of Rs. 4.91 crore. The percentage of agricultural sector is 25.6 per cent which is a little more than industrial sector which is 22.9 per cent. SBI gives more priority towards service sector because more unemployed youths are approaching the bank's for loan.

Number of Defaulters of SBI of Sample District

The total number of defaulters of State Bank of India of sample district under different sectors have been explained in Table 2.3.

Table 2.3: Sector-wise Classification of Defaulters of SBI in Ganjam district of Odisha

Sl. No.	Different Sectors	No. of Beneficiaries	Defaulters	Non-Defaulters	Percentage of Defaulters
1.	Services Sector	100	37	63	28
2.	Agricultural Sector	100	51	49	38
3.	Industrial Sector	100	44	56	34
	Total	300	132	168	100.0

Source: Compiled from questionnaires.

It reveals from Table 2.3 that the number of defaulters is less i.e. 28 per cent in service sector comparison to agricultural and industrial sectors. Agricultural sector occupies the highest percentage of defaulters than other sectors. Out of 300 sample beneficiaries of SBI in different sectors in sample district, the number of defaulters is 132 which shares 44 per cent and non-defaulters share is 56 per cent of total beneficiaries.

Finance According to the Requirements

The banking authority made finance to the sample borrowers according to the provision or according to the banking rules and regulation without considering the needs of the beneficiaries. In some cases finance made to the beneficiaries is less than requirement or in some other cases it is more than the requirements. This has been explained in Table 2.4.

Table 2.4 : Style of Finance made by the Banking Authority

Sl. No.	Style of Finance	No. of Beneficiaries	Percent-age
1.	Finance made as per the requirement of borrowers	87	29
2.	Finance made more than the requirement of borrowers	12	04
3.	Finance made less than the requirement of borrowers	201	67
	Total	300	100

Source: Compiled from questionnaires.

For the purpose of study, the style of finance made by banks has been divided into three categories, i.e. finance according to the needs of borrowers, finance below the needs of the borrowers and finance more than the needs of the borrowers. From Table 2.4 of reveals that out of the 300 sample borrowers of Ganjam district of Odisha only 12 borrowers are able to get more than the requirement of finance which constitute only 4 per cent. The major beneficiaries, i.e. 201 numbers which constitute 67 per cent are able to get finance less than the requirements of finance. It has been seen that banks always try to sanction finance the customers less than their requirements. About 29 per cent of beneficiaries of sample districts meet the finance as per their requirements. It has been seen that banks finance those beneficiaries who are able to pay their dues in times and fulfil the norms and criterion of banks.

Conclusions

The growth rate of service sector is faster than any other sector in India. It constitutes more than 50 per cent of the total GDP in the country. We cannot neglect the success of service sector in India which is due to the availability of vast skilled labours. India gained a lot from the LPG model as its GDP increased to 7.5 per cent in 2009-10. India ranks fourth in market capitalization. On the other side agriculture sector has been and still backbone of the Indian economy. It plays a vital role not only in providing food and nutrition to the people but also in the supply of raw materials to industries and to export trade. But after globalization, condition of agriculture has not improved. The share of agriculture in the GDP is only 15.80 per cent. The number of landless families has increased and farmers are still committing suicides. This is due to the lowering the per capita income of the farmers, low investment, imbalance in fertilizer use, low seeds replacement rate, increasing the rural indebtedness etc. to be a negative performance on this sector.

REFERENCES

Economic Survey of India, 2010-11.

Mishra, R.C. and A.K. Panda, "Global financial Crisis and its impact on Indian Economy", *The Orissa Journal of Commerce*, Vol. XXXI, July' 2010, p. 27.

Mohan, R, "Global Financial Crisis and key risks", 2008.

Narsis. L. An Analysis of FDI inflows in service sector and it impact on Indian Economy", *The Economic Challenger*. No. 12. Issue 48, July-Sept' 2010.

Sharma, Jyoti. "Globalization of India", *Economic Challenger*, No. 12, July-Sept' 2010, p. 35.

Srinivasan, G. "Service sector and its contribution to the Indian Economy", *Yojana*. New Delhi. Sept. 2011, p. 5.

The Economic Times, February 18, 2010, p. 1.

3

Innovation and Performance of Banks in Odisha Province and Koraput District

—Dr. Eswar Rao Pattnaik*

Introduction

Schumpeter has coined the term innovation to denote introduction of new idea or a new commodity in the market. The wave of liberalization, privatization and globalization in the 90s has pushed the wheels of progress forwards in India with a GDP growth rate of 8% per annum. Social vision can work wonders. In a democracy like ours the government has to focus on equity. Efficiency consideration cannot be undermined, if we have to accelerate the growth rate of the economy. We have been looking for ways to combine our concerns for equitable outcomes with our concerns for efficient utilization of resources. Creativity comes into being only, when there is a break from the past and when there is no repetition. Professor Muhammad Yunus observes that "credit is a key, a passport to explore the potential of a person. Credit was the real missing link between people and their creative potential."

There is a large body of consensus that rural financial institutions have touched the lives of people through efficient resource mobilization and credit deployment leading to integrated rural development, expansion of form output, creation of opportunities of employment, and eradication of poverty in the country. Viewed against this back-drop the

*Retd. Principal, S.B.R.G. Women's College, Berhampur.

present paper makes an effort to analyze and assess the role and effectiveness of banks in their effort to disburse credit for the development of agriculture allied sectors and industries in Odisha Province and Koraput District. The materials for the present study are furnished by 2011 census, *Economic Survey*, government of Odisha 2012-13. The work on Koraput District is based on S.W.O.T. analysis (Strengths Weaknesses Threats and Opportunities) compiled by COATS, Koraput with the help of primary data collected in all the blocks of Koraput District in 2007-08.

Features of the State of Odisha and Koraput District

The State of Odisha is rural oriented, agrarian and is slow to come out of the vicious circle of poverty, unemployment and sluggish growth rate. The State of Odisha has a population of 41,974,000 with a literacy rate of 72.90%, a sex ratio of 979 and 83.31% of its population dwell in rural areas. In striking contrast, the tribal dominant district of Koraput has a population of 13,80,000, literacy rate of 49.02%, a sex ratio of 1032 and 83.61% of its population live in rural areas.

Bank Branches in Odisha

Credit has an important component i.e quantitative dimension as reflected by number of banks, their branches, spread of banks and quantum of loans provided to different sectors of the economy. The qualitative dimension of credit is embodied in loan recovery position of banks, quality of services provided to customers, population served per branch and supervision over the end use of credit.

Table 3.1 summarizes that, there are 25 public sector banks, 11 private sector banks, 05 RRBS, 332 State Cooperative banks and 05 State Cooperative Agriculture and Research Development Banks in the State of Odisha in 2011-12. The reach of commercial banks is denoted by population per commercial branch, which comes to 13,000 in Odisha. In Tamil Nadu and Karnataka on the other hand there is one commercial bank branch per 9000 population. The geographical spread of Bank Branches is spotlighted by pattern of distribution Bank Branches in rural, semi-urban and urban areas. 55% of bank branches have their presence in rural areas, 25% of branches serve semi-urban branches and 20% of bank branches are located in urban areas.

Table 3.1 : Bank Branches in Odisha in 2011-12

No. of Banks	Types of Banks	No. of Branches
25	Public Sector Banks	2,157
11	Private Sector Banks	216
05	Regional Rural Banks	885
	Total Commercial Bank Branches	3258
	State Cooperative Banks	332
	State Cooperative Agriculture & Research Development (OSCARD) Bank & Others	05
	Total No. of Bank Branches	3595

Table 3.2 : Credit Inflow in Koraput District under Crop Production

Sl. No.	Year	Commercial Banks	Utkal Gramya Bank	Coope-rative Banks	Rupees in Lakhs
01	2004-05	724.18	1103.67	1320.85	3148.70
02	2005-06	591.77	1159.54	3045.46	4796.77
03	2007-07	782.66	1254.47	3599.48	5636.61

Source: NABARD P.LP, (2008-09).

What is alarming is the trend of commercial banks to claim 96% of increase in deposits of Odisha, while cooperative banks are making their services available in rural areas. The per capita deposit with a bank enables us to assess saving habits of an individual. There has been a quantum jump in per capita deposit in Odisha from Rs. 7205 in 2005-06 to Rs. 30,152 in 2011-12. In contrast per capita deposit in India has sharply picked up from Rs. 15,375 in 2005-06 to Rs. 51,106 in 2011-12.

Credit deposit ratio refers to ratio of loans advanced to total deposits and it spotlights the magnitude of banking activity. Official estimates suggest that for all commercial banks credit deposit ratio is 70.25%, while for cooperative banks credit deposit ratio is 15.37% in 2011-12.

Sectoral distribution of loans and advances by banks in 2011-12 highlights that, agriculture has claimed a lion's share of the loans i.e 44.01% (Rs. 14,178.86 crores). Non farm sector claims 13.29% of loans i.e. Rs. 3368.10 crores and Rs 10242 crores (42.70%) are allotted for other non- priority sectors, it follows that the mission of Banks of serving the poor and priority sector is in full swing in Odisha,

Three novel initiatives taken up by Banks in Odisha relate to credit prpvisiorvto self-Help groups, crop loans to farmers and differential rate of interest on loans for agricultural development. It is flower to the garland of achievements of banks that, 76,437 self help groups are covered under credit-linkage to SHGs, which have a membership of 8 Lakhs. Credit support of Rs. 258.60 crores have been provided to 6,817 groups in 2011-12 SHGs empower rural women, the marginalized poor, and help them cross the poverty line by loan facilities and extension services to members. Banks are playing a catalytic role in making loan available to agriculture at a lower rate of interest.

The introduction of ATM card facilities to customers is a novel step devised by Banks to facilitate cash withdrawals by customers. The dark spot in the body of banks in Odisha province is the presence of over dues of the order of 70.02% for R.R.Bs, 70.01% for Cooperative Banks and 61.08% for all Banks in 2011-12. Mounting over dues of banks may be checked by penalty measures, for willful be default of loan, while genuine loan default may be considered with sympathy. Sufficient recovery officials may be recruited in banks to provide expertise and advice to farmers on technology matters in agriculture supervise the end use of credit and strengthenmg field visits by recovery officials in villages.

DEVELOPMENT IN KORAPUT DISTRICT

Area under Different Crops

The estimated cultivated areas of total fruit crops, vegetables and spices are 11158 ha and 10901 ha, respectively (PLP : 2008-2009).

Progress under National Horticulture Mission

The Koraput district is covered under National Horticulture Mission (NHM). During the year 2006-07 and 2007-08, fruit orchards have been established in 1710 ha. In respect of 1667 ha of cashew, and 125 ha of banana. Flori-culture demonstration, encouragement of organic farming, plantation of medical sapling, micro-irrigation are among the other achievements.

Strengths, Opportunities, Weakness and Threats (SWOT) Analysis

Strengths

(*a*) The agro-climatic zones of the district are suitable for different types of fruits, vegetables, spices, coffee and flowers.

(*b*) The high and medium lands are abundantly available which can be diverted to horticultural crops.

(*c*) Enactment of Fruit Nursery Act, 1999 ensures control over Quality Producing Materials (QPM) in the private sector.

(*d*) Availability of abundant and cheap man power.

(*e*) Access to METROPOLIS LIKE Kalkota, Raipur, Visakapatnam etc. enhances possibilities of expert to nearby States and Districts.

Weakness

(a) Lack of awareness among the rural people about the benefits from N.H.M.

(*b*) Non-availability of adequate quality planting materials.

(*c*) Inadequate staff strength and weak extension network in the Horticulture Directorate.

(*d*) Poor marketing linkage and poor market infrastructure.

(*e*) Low irrigation facilities.

(*f*) Poor post-harvest management infrastructur e. g. poor economic conditions of the farmers.

Opportunities

(*a*) There has been an increasing demand for fruits, vegetables and flowers in the State which otherwise is being met by import from other States.

(*b*) There is enough scope for introduction and expansion of new crops and varities.

(*c*) Sufficient scope for establishment of processing units.

(*d*) Scope for protected cultivation of flowers, vegetables and planting materials.

(*e*) Scope to generate marketable surplus and also surplus for export.

Threats

(*a*) Exploitation of middlemen in the market chain,

(*b*) High incidence of pests and diseases.

(*c*) Uncertainty about market chain.

(*d*) Farmers do not get remunerative price.

Hence, it is proposed for farm mechanization, micro-nutrient demonstration, promotion of organic farming, land development, creation of irrigation facilities, IPM and INM training, construction of godown, formation of SHG, setting up of collection centers, Nursery Development, Marketing activities, Exposure visit to farmers, Vermi Compost, promotion of sericulture in the small and marginal fields, and innovative schemes like mushroom production and introduction to exotic vegetables.

Suggestions

Small and marginal farmers are dominant the economies of Odisha and Koraput district. Focus may be laid on this economically disadvantageous group at the time of lending money to them. The quantum of loans to the economically weaker section may be increased.

Credit should never be allowed to operate in the vacuum. Capital is a necessary condition but not a sufficient condition. It becomes abortive unless it is matched by complementary facilities like diversification of the cropping pattern from food crops to commercial crops, fruits, vegetables, spices etc. provision of insurance facilities, to the growers of paddy, ragi, niger, potato, sugarcane etc, accent on post harvest managment value addition, creation of marketing infrastructure and storage facilities. Use of organic fertilizers and establishment of bio control laboratory in Koraput district is likely to reduce pesticide hazard. In an economy where 50% of lands depend on monsoon, dry land farming and animal husbandry are the powerful tools for controlling the poverty of the farmers. Productivity of land and crops can be increased by increasing the off take of chemical fertilizers in recommended doses., promotion of form mechanization and completion of the existing irrigation projects which are not completed.

There are prevails yawning knowledge gap between laboratory research and field work by farmers. Extension officials may demonstrate the farmers, the benefits of the genetically modified seeds. Above all, the government may have to increase, investment in irrigation, agriculture and rural infrastructure.

With regard to financing of loans to SHGs, there are reported cases of farmers suicides in Andra Pradesh, due to use of coercive measures initiated by SHGs to recover loans from farmers. Hence SKS, a voluntary organization has incurred losses and Akul Vikram the man behind the creation of S.K.S was removed from his marginal status.

Conclusion

The daunting task of institutional credit is to transform static agriculture into dynamic agriculture, so that after loan recovery, the farmer has more income for investing in agriculture. Timely and cheap availability of credit to agriculture and related sectors, extension of irrigation facilities with timely supply of power strengthening of extension mechanism, diversification of cropping pattern from food crops to non-food crops provision of lands to landless, creation of wage employment schemes with passbook facilities to customers and encouragement to model farmers by training one outstanding male farmer and one female farmer (with cash awards) on the recent technology calls for a holistic approach to agriculture. Poverty is contained to the extent that governance improves. Above all link failures in computer operations banks may be minimized and manual power may be used to meet customer's claims.

REFERENCES

B. Pattnaik Eswar Rao "Financial Sector Reforms and Performance of Banks in India" In: Financial Institutions and Reforms, Rajib Lochan Panigrahi (Ed.), Discovery Publishing House, New Delhi, 2010.

District at a glance, Odisha, 2014.

Economic Survey 2012-13, Government of Odisha.

Mishra R.N. and G. Chandrayya "Micro Finance for Agricultural Development", Discovery Publishing House, New Delhi, 2010.

National Agriculture Development Programme (NADP)/ Rastriya Krishi Vikash Yojna, C.O.A.T.S. (RKVY) Koraput 2008.

Rajib Lochan Panigrahy "Financial Institutions and Reforms, Discovery Publishing House New Delhi, 2010.

Tribal Studies *A Journal of C.O.A.T.S.* 2013 Council of Analytical Tribal Studies, Koraput 2013, published by COATS, 2013.

4

Balanced Scorecard: An Integrated Approach to Improving Service Quality Management in Banks

—Dr. G.A. Narasimham*

Introduction

The Balanced Scorecard is a management system that enables organizations to clarify their vision and strategy and translate them into action. A prerequisite for implementing a Balanced Scorecard is a clear understanding of the organizations vision and strategy. The basis for the vision and the strategy should be the holistic view and the information the management receives during systematic strategy work. The strategy of the organization is quantified into measures or Key Performance Indicators (KPIs). The measures can be derived from the strategy using Critical Success factors (CSFs) or alternatively using strategy maps. The key properties of each of the measures in a Balanced Scorecard are also defined.

In the technical implementation phase the visions, strategies, critical success factors, measures etc. are entered into the system. The technical implementation steps include; installation of the software, training, building of the scorecards, setting target and alarm levels, setting data consolidation rules as well as defining graphs and possible customized reports. The Balanced Scorecard system is integrated to operational IT systems, databases and/or data

*Lecturer in Commerce, Government Degree College, Rampachodavaram, E.G. Distt, Andhra Pradesh.

warehouses such as financial reporting systems, Enterprise Resource Planning (ERP) systems or Customer Relationship Management (CRM) systems.

The benefits from the balanced scorecard are realized when the balanced scorecard is used in day-to-day operations. Data update, analysis and reporting are performed regularly within the management and reporting processes. From time to time it is also necessary to refine the balanced scorecard. The balanced scorecard should be a standard tool used by the management team in their strategy work.

Concept of Balanced Scorecard

The balanced scorecard serves as a measurement system, a strategic management system, and a communication tool. By definition, the balanced scorecard is a strategic measurement and management system capable of translating an organization's mission and strategy into a comprehensive set of measures. It can assist the organization to focus on issues before they become problems, transform data into actionable information and manage performance for all strategic objectives. The balanced scorecard translates strategy into objectives and measures in four perspectives; Internal Service Process Perspective, Learning, Innovation and Growth Perspective, Customer Relations Perspective and Financial Perspective.

Customer Relations Perspective

In choosing certain measures for this perspective, we must answer the questions like how do our customers see us? How do customers rate our performance? Customer surveys can serve as a measure of satisfaction. We address the following dimensions of Quality, Accessibility, Acceptability and Continuity.

Internal Service Process Perspective

In this perspective, we identify and develop measures for the key processes that we must excel at in order to meet patient/ customer expectations. For example, measuring and monitoring Turn-Around-Time (TAT) can identify opportunities to improve pre-analytical, analytical or post-analytical processes. We address the following dimensions of quality, effectiveness, appropriate-ness, and safety.

Learning, Innovation and Growth Perspective

The measures in this perspective are the enablers of the other three perspectives. They are the foundation of the balanced scorecard. Once the measures for the internal service processes and customer relations have been established, certain skill gaps will become apparent. The measures designed for the Learning and Growth perspective will close that gap. Measurements may include: training hours, employee satisfaction. We address the following dimensions of quality; competence and participation.

Financial Perspective

The measures in this perspective tell us whether the strategy execution is leading to improved results; are we meeting operational and financial targets? Are the department's goals, implementation, and execution contributing to the bottom-line? Examples of measures are workload, supply costs, and employee paid hours. We address the following Dimension of quality and efficiency in services.

NON-FINANCIAL PERSPECTIVE

Customer Perspective

The customers' perspective is observed by conducting a survey through a well designed structured questionnaire and obtained responses from a sample of 100 customers of the bank.

Table 4.1 : Duration of Customers Association with the Bank

Duration	Number of Respondents	Percentage
1-6 months	23	23
1 year	7	7
2-3 years	42	42
>3 years	28	28
TOTAL	100	100

Inference

Seventy percent of the customers are loyal customers as they are attached with the branch of the bank for more than two years. This indicates that bank is able to retain its customers successfully by maintaining and delivering quality services.

Forty-eight percent of the customers feels that the rating should around 5 to 7. This indicates that the customers are satisfied with the products and services offered by the bank (Table 4.2).

Table 4.2 : Satisfaction Level of Customers Towards the Bank Products on a Scale of 1-10

Rating Scale	Number of Respondents	Percentage
1-5	26	26
5-7	48	48
8-9	16	16
10	10	10
TOTAL	100	100

Fifty four percent of the customers opted for quick option. This clearly shows that the employees of the bank are quick in responding to the problems of the customers by delivering quality services (Table 4.3).

Table 4.3: Customers' Opinion About the Promptness in Services

Promptness in service	Number of Respondents	Percentage
Quick	54	54
Very quick	16	16
Slow	0	0
Average	30	30
TOTAL	100	100

The study shows that the customers rated the efficiency of the bank around 8 to 9 in a scale of 10. This indicates that the bank is able to handle queries and operations in a less time.

Table 4.4: Opinion on Efficiency of Meeting the Customers' Requirements by Bank on a Scale of 1-10

Rating	Number of Respondents	Percentage
1-5	10	10
5-7	24	24
8-9	37	37
10	29	29
TOTAL	100	100

Table 4.5 clearly indicate that all the customers are totally satisfied with the employees of the branch of the bank. It indicates the friendly approach of the employees and their good relationship with the customers. This shows that the employees receive some sort of training towards their behaviour with the customers.

Table 4.5: Customers Opinion about the Bank Employee's Assistance

Response	Number of Respondents	Percentage
Yes	100	100
No	0	0
TOTAL	100	100

Forty-four percent of the customers are of the opinion that the employees of the bank respond quickly to them, but 49% say that they are just satisfied with the employees responding to them as their response to this question was moderate. Still it indicated that customers are happy with the way the employees respond to them (Table 4.6).

Table 4.6: Customer's Opinion about the Responsiveness of the Bank Employees

Response	Number of Respondents	Percentage
Quick response	44	44
Slow response	7	7
No response	0	0
Moderate response	49	49
TOTAL	100	100

Sixty percent of the customers are of the opinion that the bank has a good ambiance with provides good facilities and environment which enable them to swiftly complete their transactions. Thus here ambiance of the bank indicates the technology used and the layout planned to assist their customers (Table 4.7).

Table 4.7: Customers Response Towards Ambience of the Bank

Response	Number of Respondents	Percentage
Yes	60	49
No	13	23
Can't say	27	28
TOTAL	100	100

Seventy-three percent of the customers have expressed their opinion of opting for E-Banking services. Table 4.8 indicates that they know how to utilize the banking services through net and other electronic media. The bank takes classes for their customers to make them educated about e- banking if they are willing to know about it.

Table 4.8: Response Regarding Customers Opting for e-banking Services

Response	Number of Respondents	Percentage
Yes	27	27
No	73	73
TOTAL	100	100

Thirty-four percent of the customers feel that charges levied by the bank are moderately affordable, at the same time they are willing to pay the charges as they feel that they are getting what they expected (Table 4.9).

Table 4.9: Customers perception towards the affordability of fee charged by the bank

Affordability	Number of Respondents	Percentage
Affordable	26	26
Not-affordable	19	19
Moderately affordable	34	34
Highly affordable	21	21
TOTAL	100	100

Value Systems Followed by the Bank

A value system plays a very important role in the activities related to internal perspective. It determines the rules and regulations that are to be followed by the bank. The value system determines the policies that the bank follows in order to provide good security to the money invested by its customers. Each and every organization tries to communicate its value system to the public to prove that the organization is following fair practices to carry on its activities. The value systems that the bank follows are mentioned below:

1. BFPC
2. Code of commitment
3. Model policies
    - Collection of dues and repossessions of securities
    - Cheque collection policies
    - Compensation policies
    - Redresses of customer grievances.

Therefore from the banks point of view this becomes a critical success factor as because of the value system the bank is successful to provide the following:

A. Bank is able to inculcate trust and confidence among the public thus attracting new customers,

B. Bank is able to retain its existing customers in this tough completion environment by increasing the loyalty of its customers.

Activities and Time Norms

The organization is following some standards to cope up with the current competition in banking industry. As in this industry almost all services and products rendered by different players are same, there should be some thin line of differentiation in order to survive. The only way that an organization can differentiate itself is by providing quality services as quickly as possible within a very short span of time.

The time standards are been fixed by the management to fulfil the following:

1. Provide prompt services to the customer in order to increase customer satisfaction.
2. Minimizing the customers waiting time at the branch.
3. To create a provision to serve more number of customers within a day or during a particular period of time.
4. Increase the efficiency of the employees.

Thus all the above mentioned activities can be measured on the following criteria:

- Increase in the number of new customers.
- Increase in the number of loyal customers.

Employees Targets and Evaluation

This is a very important aspect dealt in the internal perspective of an organization. It is through the employees that the organization promises to deliver its services and promote its product. If the employees are unsatisfied and inefficient then it would be the failure of the organization. Thus concentration should be laid upon the employees as well as they are the main pillars of the service industry.

The Bank has two types of employees who are as follows:

(1) **Employees elected through IBA:** Employees who are elected through the IBA or the Indian Bank Associates are not given any targets. They are into pure operations job in the bank; they do not have any sales targets. Their salaries are fixed and are not entitled to any incentives. They are rated according to their performance. Their performance is measured by the time taken by them to do an activity. Usually there are no incentives to them but they expect promotions which are usually vertical to the hierarchy.

(2) **Employees elected through the bank mainly known as contract employees.** These are the employees elected by the bank itself. Their existence in the bank is determined only through their performance. If they perform they are there or else they are sacked off from their jobs. They are assigned targets. Their performance is measured according to the time taken and also to the extent of targets attained by them. Apart from the salary received they are also paid incentives on the basis of targets attained by them.

Note:

A. The risks and responsibilities are equally distributed among different categories of employees.

B. Employee's targets are set by the TVP department which is purely engaged in the marketing of banking products and third party products.

C. The targets are first to be achieved in volumes i.e. in Rs, then the number i.e. number of application received and numbers of customers increased are considered.

Thus here employees efficiency, responsiveness, employee satisfaction etc. becomes a means of measurement.

Communication

Through proper communication the following advantages were examined:

(1) There was an increase in customer satisfaction.

(2) Trust and importance were inculcated among its customers to increase their loyalty.

(3) Facilitating proper coordination among the employees to facilitate Cross Selling.

Financial Perspective

Financial perspective is viewed by taking the views of the Branch Manager. It depends upon the branch manager how he fixes his targets to meet his assigned targets. The branch manager views his targets on two prospective which are as follows:

1. *Amount of business generated:* The branch manager usually targets to achieve the assigned targets,but in order to attain them the targets assigned were divided into three parts:
   - *Minimally successful:* This indicates the minimum target to be achieved by the branch manager. Here the branch manager is expecting

to achieve minimum of 80% of the targets assigned.

- *Fully successful:* This indicates that the branch manager is fully successful when he attains the assigned target i.e. 100%
- *Exceeds fully successful:* This indicates that the manager aims to achieve more than the targets assigned. Here the manager aims to achieve 110%-120% of the targets assigned.

2. *Increased number of customers and applications:* Usually after attaining the targets in revenue basis it's now time for the manager to concentrate upon the numbers. Thus in this process it was known that the manager was expecting a growth in number of applications and customers up to 20% per annum. He was expecting an additional increase in revenue of 30%-40% per annum with an increase of 20% of applications and customers per annum.

Conclusion

Thus from the research and analysis done on the possibility of implementation of balance score card in an bank it can be concluded that there are many current practices that are catering to the fulfilment of customer needs, providing them satisfaction, increase in employee productivity and deploying fair practices in all the services being provided by the bank and it was observed that the Critical Success Factor (CSFs) and Key Performance Indicators (KPIs) that are identified are in alignment with the corporate objectives of the bank. Implementation of balance score card at all levels of the bank, identifying some more critical success factors, Key performance indicators, would reap those benefits and helps them to measure their performance in a more efficient way and facilitates provision of better services to its customers.

REFERENCES

'Communicating and Controlling Strategy: An Empirical Study of the Effectiveness of the Balanced Scorecard' by Mary A. Malina of Naval Postgraduate School - Graduate School of Business & Public Policy and Frank H. Selto of University of Colorado at Boulder.

'Implementation of Balance Score Card in Chinese Commercial Bank of Communications (Bocom)'.

'Measurements & Balanced Scorecard' (Toronto SPIN) by Mark Kozak-Holland.

'Seven Challenges for the Implementation of Balanced Scorecard in Hospitals' by Bruno Folly Guimaraes E Silva of Tata Consultancy Services (Institute of Economics, Federal University of Rio de Janeiro).

'The balance score card Executing Strategy for Breakthrough Results' by Dr. David P. Norton, President *Balanced Scorecard Collaborative/Palladium.*

A paper submitted on 'Using the Balanced Scorecard as a Control System for Monitoring and Revising Corporate Strategy' by Dennis Campbell of Harvard Business School, Srikant Qatar (Harvard Business School), Susan Cohen Kulp (George Washington University School of Business; George Washington University - Department of Accountancy) and V.G. Naraynan (Harvard Business School).

5

Internet Banking in Indian Scenario

—T. Deepthi*

Introduction

Banks have traditionally been in the forefront of harnessing technology to improve their products, services and efficiency. The modern age banking customers often transacts through their 'friendly device' that enables them to conduct their bank transactions, trade on the stock exchange, buy their groceries, pay their children's school fee and taxes to the governments through a click of a button. Through their 'friendly device' they open accounts with banks to make the payments, and also carry out transactions at any of the multiple self-service outlets that have been started by their banks.

Today all the above and still more sophisticated services are made available to people through that 'friendly device' called **'Internet',** which is now identified as ubiquitous communication tool that made its debut in 1983. The Internet is a global web of computer networks, which allowed instantaneous and decentralized global communication possible. Rapid usage of Internet is associated with the development of the user-friendly World Wide Web and web browser software such as Netscape Navigator and Microsoft Internet Explorer.

*Lecturer in Commerce Department, ASD Government Degree College for Women, Kakinada.

In the present scenario, most of the business organizations are using the internet for a variety of communication tasks, such as promotion of consumer awareness and interest, providing information and consultation, facilitating two-way communications with customers through e-mail, stimulating product trial and enabling customers to place orders. In order to avail the benefits that are accrued through using Internet, financial institutions like banks are transforming themselves and conducting their business electronically. This transformation from normal banking to electronic banking enabled customers to transact online, while saving on various factors.

Banking through Internet

In the ever changing global scenario, banking business proved to be agile in adopting latest technology to improve its services and efficiency. Banks have evinced interest in delivering value added products and services with the help of rapidly evolving electronic and tele-communication technologies. Amidst these changes, Internet banking evolved in the mid 1990s, i.e., while World Wide Web and internet began to strengthen their roots. Subsequently, dial-up connections, personal computers, tele-banking and Automated Teller Machines (ATMs) became the order of the day in most of the developed countries. Many banking organizations in the US and Europe started providing banking services through Internet.

Internet banking is a web-based service that allows the banks authorized customer to access their account information. In this system, customers are allowed to log on to the bank's website with the help of identification issued by the bank and a Personal Identification Number. Banks replies the user and enables him to access the desired services. Often, the range of products and services offered by each bank on internet varies widely in terms of content. It is observed that Internet banking is offered as a value added service by most of the banks. Owing to the convenience offered by Internet banks, new banks which do not exist physically but conduct their business through Internet have emerged. These are known as 'Virtual Banks' or 'Internet Only' banks.

On the other hand normal banking activities still persist in developing countries like India, where the Internet penetration levels are low. Banking, essentially a service oriented business organization, buys the raw materials or stock-in-trade in the form of deposits and sells the same by way of loans and advances. Hence the bank's functions primarily aim at meeting the saving - credit requirements of a society. But the universal realization in recent years that banks have to play a crucial role in the development process of a country has brought sweeping change both in their organizational as well technical functions, which resulted in Internet banking or e-commerce.

With an aim to be 'customer friendly', Internet bank's products or services are divided into three types:

- **Information kiosks:** It provides information regarding various products and services offered by the bank to its customers apart from other general information. In addition customers' queries are received and answered through e-mail.
- **Basic Internet Banking:** Here, customers are allowed to open new accounts, check account balance and pay utility bills.
- **E-Commerce Banking:** Banking transactions are conducted through electronic media, wherein customers are enabled to use their accounts for transferring money, payments of various bills, purchase and sale of securities and online real time purchases and payments. Further, customers banking information is passed from web server to the bank's internet banking service through the WWW interface, to comply with customers requisites. The WWW interface and Internet banking service are significant in Internet banking transaction since they are the only media through which communication is passed

from one another, ensuring the safety of operation and customer data. The Internet banking server receives the customers' requests and passes it to the banking server, where the customer database is stored. The database provides the required information to the Internet banking server, which is then passed onto the web server through the fire wall, from where the customer is enabled to access the required information. This type of 'three tiered system', which comprises of web server, Internet banking server and customer database provides a controlled environment and helps in introducing Internet security technologies. There is also a provision for security analyzer tlict constantly monitors login attempts to log into an account.

Internet banking offers a bundle of benefits to the users who wish to reduce them expenditure on each transaction. According to a study conducted by consultants, Booz Alien & Hamilton, the cost of nn average transaction on the Internet is as low as 13 cents, compared to $1.07 through the branch bank 54 cents through the telephone and the 27 cents through the ATM and in India, an Internet banking transaction would cost 10 paise to the bank, as compared to Re. 1/- through a branch, 45 paise through ATM, 35 paise through phone banking and 20 paise through debit cards. Net banking eases transfer of money from one branch in a particular city to another branch in another city. A customer is also further enabled to open a FD account, order for an issue of demand drafts, enquire on the balance in his savings, current and FD account. He is also privileged to give instructions over the net to stop the payment on a cheque, request for a cheque book and verify whether all transactions are completed on his account and get a copy through e-mail.

Net Banks-Global Experience

Globally, banking industry did not remain untouched by the inevitable influence of Internet services. According to a research conducted by the RBI for Internet services being used by retail banks the world over, it was found that there were over 200 banks with their bank sites on the net, which is shown in the following pie diagrams.

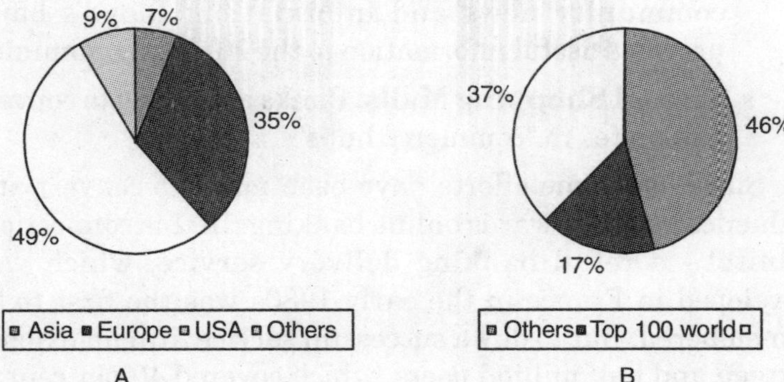

A. Split by geographical region B. Split by asset strength

The following list of services offered by banks show how online-banking is proved to be lucrative across the world and how valuable web services are becoming to retain the existing customers.

- **Putting up a sign:** Through this a bank reminds people of its services. It is also called as "maintaining zero presence" by providing information about company head quarters, telephone numbers, company logo etc.
- **Shop window:** Gives information about banks, its products, annual reports etc. Here interactivity with the customers is absent.
- **Financial Advice:** Banks interact with customers while offering advice services and answering FAQs on wealth allocation and risk tolerance to customers.
- **Selling Financial Service:** Being online, customers are allowed to register, open accounts and fill applications forms for the financial products.
- **Non-Banking activities:** Banks "off-duty" activities such as charity, welfare and social service are made available on the bank's website.
- **General Information:** A few banks are trying to fulfil the interests of housewives, students, doctors etc. For instance, local banks in America deal with local

community news and information; Lloyd's bank provides useful information to the student community.

- **Virtual Shopping Malls:** Banks are trying to convert bank sites to "commerce hubs".

Since long time efforts have been made to convert and influence people towards online banking. In this connection, Minitel - a retail banking delivery service, which was developed in France in the early 1980s was the first to be remembered. But to day a successful service firm held about sixteen and half million users, which covered 40 per cent of the adult population of the country.

On the other hand, the scenario of Net Banking in India is different, Though a modest attempt to initiate net banking is made, still there is a long way to go. Online banking report 2000, listed features of few banks like ICICI, HDFC, Citi Bank and Global Trust Bank that attempted to make 'real time banking' a reality. In this connection, ICICI bank's net banking service, Infinity offers the following features.

- It allows its customers to transfer funds into another person's account within the bank
- The customer is enabled to intimate about the loss of an ATM card over the net, while using Infinity.
- Infinity provides a facility to various corporate companies to issue letters of credit and enquire about bills sent for collection.
- "Nicknaming all accounts" is another special feature of infinity which helps to avoid remember lengthy account numbers. Another private sector bank, HDFC Bank enables its customers to have three logins, after which a new password is given. This process ensures safety to the customers. In Global Trust Bank (GTB) the entire back office work is carried out with the help of information technology.

Inward and outward clearing has been centralized. The bank also maintains disaster recovery systems at Hyderabad and Mumbai on 24/7 basis, which ensures 100 percent uptime. This provision is made apart from the state-of-art e-security to protect safety of all systems from hackers.

UTI bank's Internet banking services offer a wide range of services to the customers like balance enquiry, funds transfer, online trading, e-shopping and e-broking. It is found that the number of hits on the website of the bank exceeds one lakh per day. The bank also provides a bill payment facility through the Internet to its entire internet banking customers. In addition, the bank's web server has been constantly upgraded to meet the anticipated growth in the business.

In spite of rapid efforts to offer net banking facilities, the Indian Internet banking system need to overcome many obstacles, such as operational risks, security risks, system architecture risks, reputational risks and legal risks. Though banks are striving to overcome these problems there is lot to be done towards security of net banking operations. The banks have to be technologically strong to avoid operational and security problems. They should also be prepared to handle system disruptions, system hackers, security lapses and virus attacks. They should also be familiarized with proper customer identification devices, information screening techniques and various laws that would help guide their customers. Thus, with the growing Internet awareness among customers, integration of banking services with e-commerce and entry of global banking players, Internet banking has gained enormous importance. This fact is further proved by RBI guidelines which encouraged the implementation of internet banking in India.

REFERENCES

AasWsh Sadh & Soniya Chitale, "Customer Relationship Management & the Banking Industry", *Productivity*, Vol. 42, No. 1, April-June, 2001.

Banking in the Online World RBR, Internet for the Banking and Financial Service Conference."

GTB Bank Annual Report.

ICICI Bank's Annual Report.

Nath, R., M. Akmanligil, K. Hjelm, T. Sakaguchi & T. Schultz (1998), "Electronic Commerce and the Internet: Issues, Problems and Perspectives." *International Journal of Information Management.* 18 (2).

Neela, Radhika, "Internet banking in India", *E-Business,* October 2002.

UTI Bank Annual Report.

Yesil M. "Creating the Virtual Store", crmfoundation.com.

6

Indian Banking Industry: Challenges and Opportunities

—P. Divakarrao*

Introduction

The banking industry in India has a huge canvas of history, which covers the traditional banking practices from the time of Britishers to the reforms period, nationalization to privatization of banks and now increasing numbers of foreign banks in India. Therefore, banking in India has been through a long journey. The use of technology has brought a revolution in the working style of the banks. Nevertheless, the fundamental aspects of banking i.e. trust and the confidence of the people on the institution remain the same. However, with the changing dynamics of banking business brings new kind of risk exposure. This article is a small seed to existing branch of knowledge in banking industry and is useful for bankers, strategist, policy makers and researchers.

In recent time, we has witnessed that the World Economy is passing through some intricate circumstances as bankruptcy of banking and financial institutions, debt crisis in major economies of the world and euro zone crisis. The scenario has become very uncertain causing recession in major economies like US and Europe. This poses some serious questions about the survival, growth and maintaining the sustainable development.

*Lecturer in Commerce, Government Degree College, Tuni, E.G. (Distt.)

However, amidst all this turmoil India's Banking Industry has been amongst the few to maintain resilience. The tempo of development for the Indian banking industry has been remarkable over the past decade. It is evident from the higher pace of credit expansion, expanding profitability and productivity similar to banks in developed markets, lower incidence of non-performing assets and focus on financial inclusion have contributed to making Indian banking vibrant and strong. Indian banks have begun to revise their growth approach and re-evaluate the prospects on hand to keep the economy rolling. In this paper an attempt has been made to review various challenges which are likely to be faced by Indian banking industry.

Historical Background

Bank of Hindustan was set up in 1870; it was the earliest Indian Bank. Later, three presidency banks under Presidency Bank's act 1876 i.e. Bank of Calcutta, Bank of Bombay and Bank of Madras were set up, which laid foundation for modern banking in India. In 1921, all presidency banks were amalgamated to form the Imperial Bank of India. Imperial bank carried out limited number of central banking functions prior to establishment of RBI. It engaged in all types of commercial banking business except dealing in foreign exchange.

Reserve Bank of India Act was passed in 1934 and Reserve Bank of India (RBI) was constituted as an apex body without major government ownership. Banking Regulations Act was passed in 1949. This regulation brought RBI under government control. Under the act, RBI got wide ranging powers for supervision and control of banks. The Act also vested licensing powers and the authority to conduct inspections in RBI. In 1955, RBI acquired control of the Imperial Bank of India, which was renamed as State Bank of India. In 1959, SBI took over control of eight private banks floated in the erstwhile princely states, making them as its 100% subsidiaries. It was 1960, when RBI was empowered to force compulsory merger of weak banks with the strong ones. It significantly reduced the total number of banks from 566 in 1951 to 85 in 1969. In July 1969, government nationalised 14 banks having deposits of Rs. 50 crores and above. In 1980, government acquired 6 more banks with deposits of more than Rs. 200 crores. Nationalisation of banks was to make them play the role of catalytic agents for economic growth. The Narasimha Committee report suggested wide ranging reforms for the banking sector in 1992 to introduce internationally accepted banking practices. The amendment of Banking Regulation Act in 1993 saw the entry of new private sector banks.

Banking industry is the back bone for growth of any economy. The journey of Indian Banking Industry has faced many waves of economic crisis. Recently, we have seen the economic crisis of US in 2008-09 and now the European crisis. The general scenario of the world economy is very critical. It is the banking rules and regulation framework of India which has prevented it from the world economic crisis. In order to understand the challenges and opportunities of Indian Banking Industry, first of all, we need to understand the general scenario and structure of Indian Banking Industry.

General Banking Scenario in India

The general banking scenario in India has become very dynamic now-a-days. Before preliberalizationera, the picture of Indian Banking was completely different as the Government of India initiated measures to play an active role in the economic life of the nation, and the Industrial Policy Resolution adopted by the government in 1948 envisaged a mixed economy. This resulted into greater involvement of the state in different segments of the economy including banking and finance.

The Reserve Bank of India was nationalized on January 1, 1949 under the terms of the Reserve Bank of India (Transfer to Public Ownership) Act, 1948. In 1949, the Banking Regulation Act was enacted which empowered the

Reserve Bank of India (RBI) "to regulate, control, and inspect the banks in India." The Banking Regulation Act also provided that no new bank or branch of an existing bank could be opened without a license from the RBI, and no two banks could have common directors.

Challenges faced by Indian Banking Industry

Developing countries like India, still has a huge number of people who do not have access to banking services due to scattered and fragmented locations. But if we talk about those people who are availing banking services, their expectations are raising as the level of services are increasing due to the emergence of Information Technology and competition. Since, foreign banks are playing in Indian market, the number of services offered has increased and banks have laid emphasis on meeting the customer expectations. Now, the existing situation has created various challenges and opportunity for Indian Commercial Banks. In order to encounter the general scenario of banking industry we need to understand the challenges and opportunities lying with banking industry of India.

Rural Market

Banking in India is generally fairly mature in terms of supply, product range and reach, eventhough reach in rural India still remains a challenge for the private sector and foreign banks. In terms of quality of assets and capital adequacy, Indian banks are considered to have clean, strong and transparent balance sheets relative to other banks in comparable economies in its region. Consequently, we have seen some examples of inorganic growth strategy adopted by some nationalized and private sector banks to face upcoming challenges in banking industry of India. For example recently, ICICI Bank Ltd. merged the Bank of Rajasthan Ltd. in order to increase its reach in rural market and market share significantly. State Bank of India (SBI), the largest public sector bank in India has also adopted the same strategy to retain its position. It is in the process of acquiring its associates. Recently, SBI has merged State Bank of Indore in 2010

Growth of Banking

Zhao *et al.* (2008) used a balanced panel data set covering the period of 1992-2004 and employing a Data Envelopment Analysis (DEA)-based Malmquist Total Factor Productivity (TFP) index. The empirical study indicated that, after an initial adjustment phase, the Indian banking industry experienced sustained productivity growth, which was driven mainly by technological progress. Banks' ownership structure does not seem to matter as much as increased competition in TFP growth. Foreign banks appear to have acted as technological innovators when competition increased, which added to the competitive pressure in the banking market. Finally, our results also indicate an increase in risk-taking behaviour, along with the whole deregulation process. It was found in the study of Goyal and Joshi (2011 a) that small and local banks face difficulty in bearing the impact of global economy therefore, they need support and it is one of the reasons for merger.

Some private banks used mergers as a strategic tool for expanding their horizons. There is huge potential in rural markets of India, which is not yet explored by the major banks. Therefore ICICI Bank Ltd. has used mergers as their expansion strategy in rural market. They are successful in making their presence in rural India. It strengthens their network across.geographical boundary, improves customer base and market share.

Market Discipline and Transparency

According to Fernando (2011) transparency and disclosure norms as part of internationally accepted corporate governance practices are assuming greater importance in the emerging environment. Banks are expected to be more responsive and accountable to the investors. Banks have to disclose in their balance sheets a plethora of information on the maturity profiles of assets and liabilities, lending to sensitive sectors, movements in NPAs, capital, provisions, shareholdings of the government, value of investment in India and abroad, operating and profitability indicators, the total investments made in the equity share, units of mutual funds, bonds, debentures, aggregate advances against shares and so on.

Global Banking

It is practically and fundamentally impossible for any nation to exclude itself from world economy. Therefore, for sustainable development, one has to adopt integration process in the form of liberalization and globalization as India spread the red carpet for foreign firms in 1991. The impact of globalization becomes challenges for the domestic enterprises as they are bound to compete with global players. If we look at the Indian Banking Industry, then we find that there are 36 foreign banks operating in India, which becomes a major challenge for Nationalized and private sector banks. These foreign banks are large in size, technically advanced and having presence in global market, which gives more and better options and services to Indian traders.

Financial Inclusion

Financial inclusion has become a necessity in today's business environment. Whatever is produced by business houses, that has to be under the check from various perspectives like environmental concerns, corporate governance, social and ethical issues. Apart from it to bridge the gap between rich and poor, the poor people of the country should be given proper attention to improve their economic condition. Dev (2006) stated that financial inclusion is significant from the point of view of living conditions of poor people, farmers, rural non-farm enterprises and other vulnerable groups. Financial inclusion, in terms of access to credit from formal institutions to various social groups. Apart from formal banking institutions, which should look at inclusion both as a business opportunity and social responsibility, the author conclude that role of the self-help group movement and microfinance institutions is important to improve financial inclusion. The study suggested that this requires new regulatory procedures and de-politicisation of the financial system.

Environmental Concerns

It is quite clear from the recently formed Copenhagen Climate Council (CCC) that there is a severe need for environmental awareness among all the countries of the world. CCC published Thought Leadership Series on Climate Change which is a collection of inspirational, concise and clearly argued pieces from some of the world's most renowned thinkers and business leaders on climate change. The objective of the pieces is to assist in enhancing the public and political awareness of the actions that could have a significant impact on global emissions growth and to disseminate the message that it is time to act. The Thought Leadership Series was aimed at explaining and spreading awareness of the key elements in the business and policy response to the climate problem. The rationale for the Thought Leadership Series was to change the focus of people.

Social and Ethical Aspects

There are some banks, which proactively undertake the responsibility to bear the social and ethical aspects of banking. This is a challenge for commercial banks to consider the these aspects in their working. Apart from profit maximization, commercial banks are supposed to support those organizations, which have some social concerns. Benedikter (2011) defines Social Banks as "banks with a conscience". They focus on investing in community, providing opportunities to the disadvantaged, and supporting social, environmental, and ethical agendas. Social banks try to invest their money only in endeavours that promote the greater good of society, instead of those, which generate private profit just for a few. He has also explained the main difference between mainstream banks and social banks that mainstream banks are in most cases focused solely on the principle of profit maximization whereas, social banking implements the triple principle of profit-people-planet.

Goyal and Joshi (2011b) have concluded in their study on social and ethical aspects of Banking Industry that Banks can project themselves as a socially and ethically oriented organization by disbursement of loans merely to those organizations, which has social, ethical and environmental concerns.

Conclusion

Over the years, it has been observed that clouds of trepidation and drops of growth are two important phenomena of market, which frequently changes in different sets of conditions. The pre and post liberalization era has witnessed various environmental changes which directly affects the aforesaid phenomena. It is evident that post liberalization era has spread new colors of growth in India, but simultaneously it has also posed some challenges. This article discusses the various challenges and opportunities like rural market, transparency, customer expectations, management of risks, growth in banking sector, human factor, global banking, environmental concern, social, ethical issues, employee and customer retentions. Banks are striving to combat the competition. The competition from global banks and technological innovation has compelled the banks to rethink their policies and strategies.

REFERENCES

AI-Tamimi, H. A. H and AI-Mazrooei, F. M. "Banks' risk management: A comparison study of UAE national and foreign banks". *Journal of Risk Finance*, 8(4): 394-409, 2007.

Sensarma, R. and Jayadev, "Are bank stocks sensitive to risk management?" *Journal of Risk Finance*, 10(1): 7-22, M. 2009.

Shrieves, R. E. "The relationship between risk and capital in commercial banks". *Journal of Banking & Finance*, 16(2): 439-457, 1992.

Wolgast, M. "M&As in the financial industry: A matter of concern for bank supervisors?" *Journal of Financial Regulation and Compliance*, 9(3): 225-236, 2001.

7

Growth of Service Sector by SBI in Southern Districts of Orissa

—Dr. R.N. Misra*

The State Bank of India (SBI) which is the largest and the premier bank among the commercial banks of the country, has occupied a unique place in the Indian Money Market (IMM) as its commands more than one-third of India's banking resources. SBI came into existence on 1st July 1955 after the nationalization of the Imperial Bank of India with the help of the State Bank of India Act which was passed by the Government of India on 8th May 1955. One of the basic objectives of setting up the SBI was extension of banking facility on large scale more particularly on the rural and semi-urban areas. It plays an important role in financing the priority sectors. Service Sector is the lifeline for the social economic growth of a country. It is today the largest and fastest growing sector and contributing more to the global output and provides employment to more people than any other sector. The real reason behind the growth of the service sector is due to the increase in urbanization, privatization and more demand for intermediate and final consumer services. There has been a marked acceleration in service sector growth, especially in the post liberalization period. According to the Economic Survey 2010-11, service sector accounted for a 55.2 per cent share in the GDP, growing by

*Retd. Prof. in Commerce, Gandhi Nagar, Berhampur-760001.

ten per cent annually. At present its contribution come to more than 25 per cent of total employment of the country.

The State Bank of India is the leading Commercial Bank in the State of Orissa. It is playing an important role in supplying credit to service sector units. Eight sample districts of Southern Orissa have been taken for the purpose of the study. At present; service sector lending includes financing of transport operation, retail traders, small business, professional and small employed persons, housing loans, education loans, consumption loans etc.

Service Sector is the lifeline for the social economic growth of a country. It is today the largest and fastest growing sector and contributing more to the global output and provides employment to people in large numbers than any other sector. Availability of quality services is vital for the well being of an economy. There has been a marked acceleration in service sector growth, especially during the past liberalization period. The contribution of this sector has been manifold. According to the Economic Survey 2010-11, service sector accounted for a 55.2 per cent share in the Gross domestic Product (GDP), growing by ten per cent annually. Its share in inflows of Foreign Direct Investment (FDI) and export are also high. During the first half of 2010-11 the export growth rate is 27.4 per cent. The service sector includes wide ranges of activities like trading, transportation and communication, financial services, real estate, tourism, software industry, social and personal activities etc. One of the key service sectors in India would be health and education. They are vital to the country's economic stability.

Now service sector plays an important role and it is contributing a lion's share in economic scenario of the country. Its growth is also quite important for India. The employment elasticity in the service sector is higher than that of both agriculture and manufacturing sector. Therefore its growth generates ample opportunities in the country. At present 49 per cent of the total income of the country is shared by service sector and it generates only 26 per cent of the employment of the country. Out of the total loan of Rs.7484.49 cror es advanced by banks in Orissa during 2008-09, an amount of Rs. 3450.55 cores (46.10%) was invested on agriculture sector, followed by the service sector with investment of Rs.3383.44 cores (45.21%) and industrial sector with Rs.650.50 cores (8.69%). Service sector also provides complementary services to agriculture and acts industrial sector and as a catalyst in the growth of the entire economy which needs due consideration.

Automation Services of Banks

Information Technology (IT) and the Communication Networking Systems (CNS) have revolutionized the working of banks and financial entities all over the world. There is a need to bring about financial inclusion by using technological inputs on a massive scale to extend banking services to the remote areas. The RBI has set up an advisory group for IT Enabled Financial Inclusion to facilitate development of Information Technology solution for delivery of banking services. Leading banks have been prompt in providing efficient customer service and offering a variety of Hi-Tech banking services like Automatic Teller Machine (ATM) service, Electronic Funds Transfer (EFT) System and Real Time Gross Settlement (RTGS) system. The focus on technology will increase even more in times to come, and will add value to customer services, develop new products, strengthen risk management etc. E-banking has already become an indispensable reality for a large percentage of Indians. Some of the features make this service attractive to the user. These are

1. He can access current/savings account balance at any time/any place.
2. He can obtain charge and credit card statements.
3. He can pay bills on line.
4. He can down load amount transactions.
5. He can transfer money between accounts.

6. He can keep track of account on time.
7. He can send e-mails to the bank requesting the services.
8. He can have a flexible schedule.
9. He can also use additional services like free phone banking, ATM and payment of bill.
10. Transfer and Exchange of Foreign Currency.
11. Issue of Debit and Credit Cards.
12. Lockers Facilities Gold and Cerficates etc.

The process of computerization, which was the starting point of all technological initiatives, is reaching near completion in most of banks. All Public Sector Banks have already crossed the 70 per cent level of computerization of their business. The Reserve Bank of India (RBI) has been continuously encouraging banks to use technology based solution for increased delivery of services. The cumulative amount spent by public sector banks on automation during September 1999 to March 2009 aggregated Rs.18,168 crore registering an increase of 21 per cent over the previous year. Some of the services offered by the banks using electronic based services are Automatic Teller Machine (ATM) services, Electronic Fund Transfer (EFT) system and Real Time Gross Settlement (RTGS) system. These developments have contributed to the speed efficiency and safety of the payment system.

ATM Services

The ATM was one of the earliest electronic banking products introduced in the mid 1970s. It is used by banks for making customer dealing easier. This system is also known as Any Time Money because it allows customers to withdraw money at any time from the bank. It increases existing business and generate new business. It allows the customer to transfer money to and from accounts, deposit cheque or cash, view account information. ATM is the most convenient way to withdraw cash. ATM offers benefits to bank i.e. improved customer services, longer penetration alternative to extended hour services, less crowding at the bank. The total number of ATMs installed by the bank is 43,651 which are the 56.9 per cent of total branches i.e. 61,129 by the end of March 2008. The SBI established 8,433 ATMs out of 15,105 branches by the end of March 2008 in India which covered only 55.8 per cent.

Table 7.1: Number of Branches and ATMs of SBI in India, Orissa and South Orissa as on March 2008

	India		Orissa		South Orissa	
Banks	Branches	ATMs	Branches	ATMs	Branches	ATMs
SBI	15105(100)	8433(59)	582(100)	291(49.9)	157(100)	60(38.2)

Source: *Daily Oriya News Paper Sambad*, Dated 6.1.2008.

The number of SBI branches in Orissa is 582 as on March 2008, out of which 157 branches are in South Orissa which constitutes 27 per cent of total branch. There are 291 ATMs in Orissa where as in South Orissa its number is only 60 which cover 38.2 per cent only. In India, the number of ATMs is 8433 which covers 60 per cent of total branch.

Electronic Fund Transfer

The Electronic Funds Transfer (EFT) continuously transfers money from one account to another. In this system, the receiver and the sender of funds may be located in different cities and may even bank with different banks. This system also makes possible payments for credit cards, private level cards, charge cards, payments of insurance premium etc. The main features are quick and safe movement of deposit money. To encourage the use of electronic mode of payment, the Reserve Bank of India (RBI) waived the processing charges for all electronic payment systems operated by it for another year. In terms of value, transactions increased to Rs. 8,31,159 crore during the year 2007-08 as compared to Rs. 1,08,714 crore in the previous year. The electronic fund transfer increased more than seven times during 2007-08 over the previous year.

Real Time Gross Settlement System

The RTGS system has several unique features. It is a single and all India system, with the settlement being effected in Mumbai. The payments are settled transaction by transaction. It is fully secure system, which uses digital signatures for safe and secure message transmission. Under this system, inter bank transactions and net clearing transactions and customer based interbank transactions can be settled. Thus it provides less risk based funds transfer for both banks and for their customers. The RTGS system has gained significance in terms of both coverage #nd value of transactions over the past four years. At the end of May 2008, 47,608 branches had RTGS connectivity and had handled transactions valued at Rs. 2,73,18,330 crore.

Sector-wise Finance made by SBI in Southern Districts of Orissa

South Orissa produces a variety of crops like cereals, pulses, oil seeds, spices, vegetables etc. Rice is the single major crops produced in south Orissa. The total population of the South Orissa according 2001 census is 82.43 lakhs which forms 22.41 per cent of the state total population. It is formed one third of total geographical area. There are number of commercial banks, Cooperative banks and

RRBs in South Orissa. SBI is the largest and premier bank among the commercial banks of the Orissa as well as South Orissa. SBI has 157 no of branches in South Orisa. The total finance made by SBI for the development of service sector in South Orissa during the period of 2002-03 to 2009-10 is illustrated in Table 7.2.

Sector-wise finance made by SBI in Sothern Districts of Orissa for the period 20 02-03 to 2009-10 has been given in Table 7.2.

Table 7.2: Financed by SBI towards Different Sectors in Southern Districts of Orissa during the period 2002-03 to 2009-10

(Rs. in crores)

Sl. No.	Year	Service Sector	Agriculture Sector	Industrial Sector	Total Advance
01	2002-03	348.98 (73.61)	81.91 (17.28)	43.17 (09.11)	474.06 (100)
02	2003-04	194.76 (80.22)	25.88 (10.66)	22.15 (09.12)	242.79 (100)
03	2004-05	126.83 (77.99)	23.43 (14.40)	12.37 (07.61)	162.63 (100)
04	2005-06	135.67 (73.64)	39.09 (21.22)	09.48 (05.14)	184.24 (100)
05	2006-07	113.63 (56.53)	69.47 (34.56)	17.90 (08.91)	201.00 (100)
06	2007-08	137.97 (54.49)	83.96 (33.16)	31.25 (12.35)	253.18 (100)
07	2008-09	240.83 (71.08)	71.03 (20.97)	26.94 (07.95)	338.80 (100)
08	2009-10	183.58 (66.97)	71.88 (26.22)	18.64 (06.81)	274.10 (100)
	Total	1482.25 (69.56)	466.65 (21.90)	181.90 (08.54)	2130.80 (100)

Source: Records of SBI Regional Office, Berhampur.

Note: Bracket Indicate the percentage.

The trends of advance pattern of the bank during the study period have been shown in Table 7.2. It is reveals from the table that out of 2130.89 crore financed by SBI in Southern Orissa for the period 2002-03 to 2009-10. Service Sector financed for Rs. 1482.25 crore which contribute 69.56 per cent of total finance and followed by agriculture and industrial sector of Rs.466.65(21.65 per cent) crore and 181.90 (8.54 per cent) crore respectively. It has been seen that service sector financed more than 54 per cent in all the year of the study. In except first three year agriculture sector financed more than 20 per cent during the study period. In industrial sector finance made by SBI is only 8.54 per cent Rs. 181.90 during the study period. In the year 2007-08, SBI has financed Rs. 31.25 crore which share is 12.35 per cent and the remaining years financed below 10 per cent of total finance. It has been seen that banks are interested to finance more to the service sector than in comparison to other sectors.

Conclusions

In addition to the main services of keeping deposits and making advances, the bank also renders a number of other services grouped, under miscellaneous business. Those are Government Business, Remittances, Bills Transactions, Gift Cheques, Letter of Credit, Bank Guarantees, Safe Custody/ Deposit, and Lockers Facility etc. It has been seen that service sector financed more than 54 per cent in all the year of the study. In except first three year agriculture sector financed more than 20 per cent during the study period. In industrial sector, finance made by SBI is 12.35 per cent in the year 2007-08 and the remaining years financed only below 10 per cent of total finance. It has been seen that banks are interested to finance more to the service sector than in comparison to other sectors.

8

Recent Trends in Indian Banking Industry

—Dr. Gangaiah*

Introduction

India's Rs 77 trillion (US$ 1.30 trillion)-banking industry is well at par with global standards and norms. Prudent practises and conventional framework adopted by the regulator, Reserve Bank of India (RBI), have insulated Indian banks from the global financial crisis.

The country has 87 scheduled commercial banks with deposits worth Rs. 71.6 trillion (US$ 1.21 trillion) as on 31st May, 2013. Of this, 26 are public sector banks, which control over 70 per cent of India's banking sector, 20 are private banks and 41 are foreign banks. Of the total, 41 banks are listed with a total market capitalisation of Rs.9.35 trillion (US$ 158.16 billion) as per the recent statistics.

Recent Developments

- India's leading infrastructure development and finance company Infrastructure Leasing & Financial Services Limited (IL&FS), has inked a Memorandum of Understanding (MoU) with Industrial and Commercial Bank of China (Asia) Limited (ICBC (Asia)), for mutual cooperation in infrastructure project development services and financial services related thereto.

*Lecturer in Commerce, Government Degree College, Tuni, E.G. (Distt.).

- The agreement envisages a scope of cooperation between the two financial entities for providing infrastructure project development services, including financial services relating thereto, trade, corporate banking, investment banking and treasury related services, debt raising, advisory and other form of permissible economic cooperation for such projects across Northern and Eastern Asia and is expected to facilitate more business opportunities for both the institutions in these geographies.
- Meanwhile, Standard Chartered Bank has announced that it will buy US-based Morgan Stanley's domestic private wealth management business. The deal, completed in the of 2013, would boost Standard Chartered's private wealth assets under management by 25 per cent or about US$ 750 million.
- Marking another milestone in achieving financial inclusion, Vodafone India and ICICI Bank have partnered to launch a mobile money transfer and payment service, M-Pesa. The service will allow customers to transfer money to any mobile phone in India, remit funds to bank accounts, deposit and withdraw cash from designated outlets, pay utility bills, and shop at select merchant establishments. The new service will initially be offered in West Bengal, Bihar and Jharkhand through 8,300 authorised agents. It will be made available across India by 2014-15.
- Public sector lender SBI intends to make a strong position in refinance market in 2013. The bank offers lowest lending rates for buying homes. The fast growing market of home loans transferred from other banks consists 25 per cent of the total home loans disbursed by the bank in FY13. SBI made Rs 30,000 crore (US$ 5.08 billion) of home loans in 2012-13.

- Meanwhile, US-based Customers Bancorp Inc (CUBI) has plans to infuse US$ 51 million in multiple securities of Religare Enterprises Ltd. Religare is currently aspiring for a banking licence to enter the banking industry.

The Banking sector has been immensely benefited from the implementation of superior technology during the recent past, almost in every nation in the world. Productivity enhancement, innovative products, speedy transactions seamless transfer of funds, real time information system, and efficient risk management are some of the advantage derived through the technology. Information technology has also improved the efficiency and robustness of business processes across banking sector. India's banking sector has made rapid strides in reforming itself to the new competitive business environment. Indian banking industry is the midst of an IT revolution. Technological infrastructure has become an indispensable part of the reforms process in the banking system, with the gradual development of sophisticated instruments and innovations in market practices.

IT in Banking

Indian banking industry, today is in the midst of an IT revolution. A combination of regulatory and competitive reasons has led to increasing importance of total banking automation in the Indian Banking Industry. The bank which used the right technology to supply timely information will see productivity increase and thereby gain a competitive edge. To compete in an economy which is opening up, it is imperative for the Indian Banks to observe the latest technology and modify it to suit their environment. Information technology offers a chance for banks to build new systems that address a wide range of customer needs including many that may not be imaginable today. Following are the innovative services offered by the industry in the recent past:

Electronic Payment Services - E Cheques

Nowadays we are hearing about e-governance, e-mail, e-commerce, e-tail etc. In the same manner, a new technology is being developed in US for introduction of e-cheque, which will eventually replace the conventional paper cheque. India, as harbinger to the introduction of e-cheque, the Negotiable Instruments Act has already been amended to include: Truncated cheque and E-cheque instruments.

Real Time Gross Settlement (RTGS)

Real Time Gross Settlement system, introduced in India since March 2004, is a system through which electronics instructions can be given by banks to transfer funds from their account to the account of another bank. The RTGS system is maintained and operated by the RBI and provides a means of efficient and faster funds transfer among banks facilitating their financial operations. As the name suggests, funds transfer between banks takes place on a 'Real Time' basis. Therefore, money can reach the beneficiary instantaneously and the beneficiary's bank has the responsibility to credit the beneficiary's account within two hours.

Electronic Funds Transfer (EFT)

Electronic Funds Transfer (EFT) is a system whereby anyone who wants to make payment to another person/company etc. can approach his bank and make cash payment or give instructions/authorization to transfer funds directly from his own account to the bank account of the receiver/beneficiary. Complete details such as the receiver's name, bank account number, account type (savings or current account), bank name, city, branch name etc. should be furnished to the bank at the time of requesting for such transfers so that the amount reaches the beneficiaries' account correctly and faster. RBI is the service provider of EFT.

Electronic Clearing Service (ECS)

Electronic Clearing Service is a retail payment system that can be used to make bulk payments/receipts of a similar nature especially where each individual payment is of a repetitive nature and of relatively smaller amount. This facility is meant for companies and government departments to make/receive large volumes of payments rather than for funds transfers by individuals

Automatic Teller Machine (ATM)

Automatic Teller Machine is the most popular devise in India, which enables the customers to withdraw their money 24 hours a day 7 days a week. It is a devise that allows customer who has an ATM card to perform routine banking transactions without interacting with a human teller. In addition to cash withdrawal, ATMs can be used for payment of utility bills, funds transfer between accounts, deposit of cheques and cash into accounts, balance enquiry etc.

Point of Sale Terminal

Point of Sale Terminal is a computer terminal that is linked online to the computerized customer information files in a bank and magnetically encoded plastic transaction card that identifies the customer to the computer. During a transaction, the customer's account is debited and the retailer's account is credited by the computer for the amount of purchase.

Tele Banking

Tele Banking facilitates the customer to do entire non-cash related banking on telephone. Under this devise Automatic Voice Recorder is used for simpler queries and transactions. For complicated queries and transactions, manned phone terminals are used.

Electronic Data Interchange (EDI)

Electronic Data Interchange is the electronic exchange of business documents like purchase order, invoices, shipping notices, receiving advices etc. in a standard, computer processed, universally accepted format between trading partners. EDI can also be used to transmit financial information and payments in electronic form.

Challenges faced by Banks, vis-a-vis, IT Implementation

It is becoming increasingly imperative for banks to assess and ascertain the benefits of technology implementation. The fruits of technology will certainly taste a lot sweeter when the returns can be measured in absolute terms but it needs precautions and the safety nets. The increasing use of technology in banks has also brought up 'security' concerns. To avoid any mishaps on this account, banks ought to have in place a well-documented security policy including network security and internal security. The passing of the Information Technology Act has come as a boon to the banking sector, and banks should now ensure to abide strictly by its covenants. An effort should also be made to cover e-business in the country's consumer laws. Some are investing in it to drive the business growth, while others are having no option but to invest, to stay in business. The choice of right channel, justification of IT investment on ROI, e-governance, customer relationship management, security concerns, technological obsolescence, mergers and acquisitions, penetration of IT in rural areas, and outsourcing of IT operations are the major challenges and issues in the use of IT in banking operations.

Conclusion

Indian banking system will further grow in size and complexity while acting as an important agent of economic growth and intermingling different segments of the financial sector. It automatically follows that the future of Indian banking depends not only in internal dynamics unleashed by ongoing returns but also on global trends in the financial sectors. Indian Banking Industry has shown considerable resilience during the return period. The second generation returns will play a crucial role in further strengthening the system. The banking today is re-defined and re-engineered with the use of Information Technology and it is sure that the future of banking will offer more sophisticated services to the customers with the continuous product and process innovations. Thus, there is a paradigm shift from the seller's market to buyer's market in the industry and finally it affected at the bankers level to change their approach from "conventional banking to convenience banking" and "mass banking to class banking". The shift has also increased the degree of accessibility of a common man to bank for his variety of needs and requirements. Adoption of stringent prudential norms and higher capital standards, better risk management systems, adoption of internationally accepted accounting practices and increased disclosures and transparency will ensure the Indian Banking industry keeps pace with other developed banking systems.

REFERENCES

Bajaj, Kamlesh & Dehjaji; *E-Commerce*, Tata McGraw-Hill Publications Co. Ltd., New Delhi, 2005.

Gupta, B.P., V.K. Vashistha, H.R. Swami, *Banking and Finance*, Ramesh Book Depot, Jaipur-New Delhi (2008).

Various issues of *Business Week, The Economist, Business Today, The Economic Times* and *Financial Express*.

Verma, S.B.; *E-Banking and Development of Banks*, Deep & Deep Publications, New Delhi, 2008.

9

Efficiency in Electronic Banking

—Dr. Rama Krishna*

Introduction

The banking industry has become stronger after the deep crisis of the eighties and it has been experiencing an increasing concentration through mergers of large and medium size banks. As it is today we found five large banks (with a market share of 10% and above), eight banks with a market share between 2% and 6% and twelve small banks (with a market share below 1%). Several of these banks are established as open corporations (54% of total banks remain as branches of international banks. Another characteristic of the banking industry is the adequate level of solvency and the good supervision and prudential regulation from the economic authority.

The strength of the banking system was tested with the "tequila effect" in 1994 and the recent Asian crisis. Until today the system is working and all the banks have fulfilled the liquidity, solvency and capitalization requirements. Nevertheless, there is always a concern related to the efficiency reached by the banks. Especially when one of the reasons given by the owners to merge two banks is efficiency. This paper analyzes the bank efficiency and its determinants using both profit and cost function. During the past 5 years,

*Lecturer in Commerce, P.R. Govt. College (A), Kakinada-533 001, East Godavari Distrist, Andhra Pradesh.

the Internet has brought about fundamental changes in the rules of operation of the banking industry (Gunasekaran and Love, 1999). Specifically, the industry has moved rapidly to exploit the new communication/transaction channels offered by the Internet to improve their front-end Internet applications. As a result, the number of e-banking Web sites has increased rapidly (Aladwani, 2001). Currently, there are more than 11,250 e-banking sites located worldwide. In Iran alone, for example, more than 25 online banking sites are available with all of them to presentation Services.

Service Quality in E-Banking

Today, many financial services organizations are endeavoring to become customer focused. A key component of improved customer focus is the implementation of tools that allow development of better relations between banks and their customers (customer-bank relationship). Across all service industries, service quality remains a critical issue as businesses strive to maintain a comparative advantage in the marketplace (Kandampully and Duddy, 1999). Because financial services, particularly banks, compete in the marketplace with generally undifferentiated roducts, service quality becomes the primary competitive weapon (Stafford, 1996; Kim *et al.,* 1998). Easing wood and Storey (1993) report that total quality is the most important factor in the success of new financial services. Likewise, Bennett and Higgins (1988) believe that a competitive edge in banking originates almost exclusively from service quality. In general, it is conceded that banks that excel in quality service have a distinct marketing edge because improved levels of service quality relate to higher revenues, increased cross-sell ratios, higher customer retention (Bennett and Higgins, 1988), and an expanded market share (Bowen and Hedges, 1993).As discussed above, providing quality service and products to customers is essential for success and survival in today's competitive banking environment (Wang et al., 2003). Quality products and services enhance a bank's reputation, improve its customer retention, attract new customers, and increase its financial performance and profitability.

Quality Function E-Banking

QFD is a systematic process used by cross functional teams to identify and resolve the issues involved in providing products, processes, services, and strategies that enhance customer satisfaction (Gonza'lez *et al.*, 2003). Akao (1990) defines QFD as a method for defining design qualities that are in keeping with customer expectations and then translating the customer requirements into design targets and critical quality assurance points that can be used throughout the production/service development phase Gonza'lez (2001) states that QFD has two fundamental purposes to improve (1) the communication of customer requirements throughout the organization, and (2) the completeness of specifications and to make them traceable directly to customer requirements and needs. Some uniform rules concerning the use of electronic signatures and records in retail and commercial transactions may emerge as a result of recent changes in federal law. While these changes provide more legal certainty that may help promote the growth of electronic commerce, federal law leaves unresolved several important issues related to the validity of an electronic record, as well as the verification and authorization of parties who conduct electronic transactions. 1 In addition, the Automated Clearing House (ACH) system is increasingly being used as a payment system for funds transfers initiated on the Internet.

Literature Review on Service Quality in E-Banking

As a consequence of the increasing importance of modern information and communication technologies for the delivery of financial services the analysis of e-banking quality issues becomes an area of growing interest to researchers and managers (Hughes, 2003; Jayawardhena, 2004). Virtually all studies dealing with the quality of electronic financial services focus on specific aspects of the quality evaluation. To our knowledge, the study presented by Gounaris and Dimitriadis (2003) is the first attempt to investigate the service quality of e-banking portals. Based on the SERVQUAL, the author identifies three quality dimensions, namely customer care and risk reduction benefit, information benefit and interaction facilitation. These dimensions are represented by only 14 items, a fact that has to be criticized. These indicators do not fully cover all relevant facets regarding the business activities of an e-banking portal, which contradicts the idea of portals as holistic business models. For example, aspects like offering a broad spectrum of complementary products and services or the reliability of service delivery are not included. In the article, the author explores the implementation techniques of Activity-Based Costing in the banking sector on the example of an Estonian bank in order to analyze the cost structure for traditional and electronic channel transactions. Also conclusions are drawn about the profitability of e-banking transactions.

Definition

The Internet includes all related web-enabling technologies and open telecommunication networks ranging from direct dial-up, the public World Wide Web, cable, and virtual private networks (BIS-EBG, 2003). Internet banking (e-banking) is defined to include the provision of retail and small value banking products and services through electronic channels as well as large value electronic payments and other wholesale banking services delivered electronically. (BIS-EBG, 2003). Basic information e-banking/web sites that just disseminate information on banking products and services offered to bank customers and the general public; Simple transactional ebanking/web sites that allow bank customers to submit applications for different services, make queries on their account balances, and submit instructions to the bank, but do no permit any account transfers; Advanced transactional e-banking/web sites that allow bank customers to electronically transfer funds to/from their accounts pay bills, and conduct other banking transaction online. Usually, e-banking refers to types II and III.

Internet Profit Generation

E-commerce, when properly integrated into existing banking operations, can lead to substantial cost savings and higher profitability. Cost savings occur by virtue of automating customer transactions such as funds transfers, payments, account balance inquiries, etc. Strategic alliances with insurance companies, mortgage companies, and stock brokerage firms can lead to additional business opportunities that otherwise will go unrealized. Furthermore, banks are able to retain customers more effectively when offering services that are value-added. This has been clearly demonstrated in the case of Wells Fargo bank. When customers moved online with Wells Fargo, the percentage of customers taking their business elsewhere dropped 50 percent. As a result of these positive experiences with online banking, one in six of the bank's new customers are referrals from existing customers And, thus, did not cost the bank anything to acquire them (Meckbach, 1999).

Benefits of Internet and E-banking TO Banks

Cost Savings Orr (1999) states that electronic processing dramatically reduces the cost per transaction. According to DiDio (1998), the average transaction cost at a fall service bank is about $1.07. It reduces to $0.27 at an ATM and falls to about a penny if the same transaction is conducted on the web. Also, there are opportunities for banks to present customer bills electronically. The cost of delivering bills electronically is substantially ower than if the bill was in paper form delivered through the mail. Irvine (1999) states that electronic bill presentment costs 40% less than paper delivery. These cost savings can offer customers and banks alike reduced cost of banking and still provide efficient and varied services.

Customer Satisfaction

Retention is increasingly developing into key success factors in e-banking. Most importantly, profitable e-banking requires a strong focus not only on the acquisition of new customers but also on the retention of existing customers, since the acquisition costs in online banking exceed that of traditional offline business by 20-40 per cent (Reibstein, 2002; Reichheld and Schefter, 2000). Consequently, establishing long-term customer relationships is a prerequisite for generating positive customer value on the internet. The most important step in providing a sophisticated level of service through e-banking portals is to identify and measure the dimensions of portal quality. This is the basic prerequisite for an effective quality management. Thereby, a portal's market success greatly depends on a customer-oriented definition of quality. What really determines an e-banking portal's quality is the customers' expectations and demands rather than objective or technical characteristics (Zeithaml *et al.*, 2002). Therefore, in the following, we develop a model for assessing quality from the user's perspective.

The Role of e-Channels in the Banking Sector

Electronic banking (e-banking) is the newest delivery channel of banking services. The definition of e-banking varies amongst researches partially because electronic banking refers to several types of services through which a bank's customers can request information and carry out most retail banking services via computer, television or mobile phone (Daniel, 1999; Mols, 1998; Sathye, 1999). Burr, 1996, for example, describes it as an electronic connection between the bank and customer in order to prepare, manage and control financial transactions. Electronic banking can also be defined as a variety of the following platforms: (a) Internet banking (or online banking), (b) telephone banking, (c) TV-based banking, (d) mobile phone banking, and (e) PC are banking (or offline banking). In this paper, the ATM (Automated Teller Machine) channel is also added to the research.

Account Origination and Customer Verification

With the growth in electronic banking and commerce, financial institutions need to utilize reliable methods of originating new customer accounts online. Customer identity verification during account origination is important in reducing the risk of identity theft, fraudulent account applications, and unenforceable account agreements or transactions. Potentially significant risks arise when a financial institution accepts new customers through the Internet or other purely electronic channel because of the absence of the physical cues that bankers traditionally use to identify individuals.

To summarize these Assumptions, the following can be stated

1. It is possible to implement ABC in the banking sector, although the calculations system can become overly detailed to manage.
2. Electronic channels provide cost-saving for banks and their clients. In the case of Hans bank, Online bank payments are 12.5 times cheaper and offline bank payments are 30 times cheaper than the traditional transactions made in the branch Network.
3. The decrease in transaction costs is slower than expected.

The reason for this is that the existing channels cannot be closed at the same speed as new distribution channels are introduced and funds invested in their development and maintenance. As the number of transactions in branches has been steadily decreasing, the unit cost expenses related to branch transactions will increase the branches will become more focused on consulting and problem-solving than on regular transaction processing (payments, cash operations). The initial investments in e-channels IT and security solutions were high, also IT and product development require major investment at the beginning stage. We can conclude that e-channels transactions will probably become more cost-efficient for banks in a few years' time. The detailed information provided by the ABC technique can help banks to regulate and reduce some cost components. Understanding of the IT cost components of e-banking distribution channels gives an insight about the fixed and floating components of IT expenses and thus can create the preconditions for cost saving.

Online Banking in Iran Like Country

The development of online banking in Iran country reveals some common traits. In recent years, the dominant industrial strategy in Iran country is for banking groups to own both pure internet banks and more traditional banks with an internet portal, thus exploiting both business models. Internet banks that initially offered only online tools have gone over to a mixed model, using other channels as, for example, telephone banking, or financial advisors. Stand-alone internet banks are rather rare. The large majority of traditional banks have set up an internet portal to diversify their distribution channel. But in addition, many banking groups have set up separate internet banks with their own brand that function as independent entities. We examine the performance of banking groups that have set up internet banks (pure internet banks) versus banks that offer a mix of distribution channels (mixed banks). We look into the development of online banking in all cities Iran country. This enables us to expand the dataset to produce clearer evidence regarding the performance of online banking. But in addition, it allows us to contrast different banking models. This makes the results more widely applicable than studies focused on a specific market. These cities not only represent a variety of banking structures but also differ in their economic structure, and in particular in their adoption of new technologies. These external factors possibly affect the success of internet banking.

Prospects Impact of E-banking on Traditional Banking

The early conventional wisdom Internet banking would destroy the traditional banking business model and promote the entry of newcomers from the outside of the banking industry. Developing countries could have the "opportunities to leapfrog" in the adoption of e-finance on a large scale. In reality, e-banking develops fast, but not damaging as conventional wisdom projected. The notion of leapfrog has not worked in many developing countries due to various impediments. This can be verified by UNCTAD report: "Some positive signs are already visible, including a high level of acceptance of technology by customers and financial institutions....H (h) owever; most projects have not yet been deployed on a large scale." (UNCTAD 2002). It provides a comprehensive look at the status of e finance in developing countries. It covers arrange of areas related to e finance including e-banking, e-payments, e-trades, and e-credit information).

Trust as a Function of Degree of Perceived Risk

Risk has been called element that gives the trust dilemma. If there was no risk and actions could be taken with complete certainly no trust would be needed. This element of risk is particularly pronounced in electronic commerce as opposed to traditional commerce. Previous research on trust lacks on clarifying the relationship of trust and risk. Although numerous authors have recognized the importance of risk to understand trust, no consensus on its relationship with trust exists. Trust is interwoven with risk, because it reduces the risk of falling victim to opportunistic behaviour.

Perceived Security

Security is being defined as a threat creates circumstance, condition, or event with the potential to cause economic hardship to data or network resources in the form of destruction, disclosure, modification of data, denial of service, and/or fraud, waste, and abuse. Under this definition, in the context of electronic banking threats can be made either through network and data transaction attacks or through unauthorized access to the account by means of false or defective authentication. Perceived security then is the customer's perception of the degree of protection against these threats. (Kalakota and Whinston 1997).

Perceived Privacy

Privacy has been identified to be a major, if not the most critical, important to e-commerce: In our view, the single, overwhelming barrier to rapid growth of e-commerce is a lack of consumer trust that consumer protection and privacy laws will apply in cyberspace. Consumers worry, deservedly, that supposedly legitimate companies will take advantage of them by invading their privacy to capture information about them for marketing and other secondary purposes without their informed consent. A number of researchers have examined the concept of privacy from a behavioral perspective.

Perceived Trustworthiness

People make important buying decisions based, in part, on their level of trust in the product, salesperson, or the company. Similarly, electronic banking decision involves trust not simply on the transaction medium but also between the customer and the bank or the financial service provider.

Conclusion

This paper studies economic efficiency in the E-banking industry using a stochastic frontier approach. For measuring economic efficiency we used two indicators the cost and the alternative profit function. We found that banks that are open corporations tend to be more efficient in cost and profit than those banks that are branches of international banks. This result survives after controlling by size, market concentration, credit risk and economic activity. This would suggest two alternative hypotheses. The first one is related to principal agent problem. Banks, which are open corporations, are being observed closely by the market and they could be subject to take over. Therefore managers carefully handle cost and profit. On the other side foreign owners of banks, which are branches of multinational banks, tend to exert less control over the managers, with the corresponding cost and profit inefficiency. The second hypothesis is related to the type of business that these two groups are conducting. On the one hand, open corporations tend to be large banks that act as universal banks, by providing all the services permitted by the law. On the other hand, international branches tend to be small banks that are not involved in retailing banking and they are serving only to very large companies or they just do intermediate investment. Another finding supports the fact that principal agent problem is important for cost and profit efficiency is the evidence presented here on the relationship between ownership structure and efficiency.

REFERENCES

Akao, Y. (1990), *Quality Function Deployment: Integrating Customer Requirements into Product Design,* Productivity Press, and Cambridge, MA.

Aladwani, A.M. (2001), "Online banking: afield study of drivers, development challenges, and expectations", *International Journal of Information Management,* Vol. 21, pp. 213-25.

Bowen, J. and Hedges, R.B. (1993), "Increasing service quality in retail banking", *Journal of Retail Banking*, Val, 15.

BIS 2003, *Management and Supervision of Cross-border Electronic Banking Activities.*

Daniel, E. "Provision of electronic banking in the UK and Ireland," *International Journal of Bank Marketing*, 17, 2, 1999, pp. 72-82. "The Dynamo of E-Banking", *Business Week* Online, April 16,2001.

DiDio, Laura. "Beta Testers Endorse E-checks" *Computerworld* (32), 1998, p. 57.

Gunasekaran, A. and Love, P. (1999), "Current and future Directions of multimedia technology in business", *International Journal of Information Management*, Vol. 19 No. 2, pp. 105-20.

Gonza' lez, M., Quesada, G. and Bahill, T. (2003), "Improving product design using quality function Deployment: theschool furniture case in developing Countries", *Quality Engineering Journal*, Vol. 16, No. 1, pp. 47-58.

10

NPA Management in Banks—An Innovative Approach

—B.N.V. Parthasarathi*

Introduction

Non-performing assets (NPAs) pose a major threat to banks in two ways i.e., declining profits and erosion of capital base. As per the extant RBI guidelines an advance or loan given by a bank will be classified as non-performing when the principal repayment or servicing of interest is due for more than 90 days but not paid. Depending on the extent of irregularity a non-performing asset is in turn further classified into sub-standard and loss assets. The bank has to stop recognizing the income on such non performing assets on accrual basis. In other words the bank can recognize the income on such NPAs only on cash realization basis. Additionally the bank has to assess the risk in such NPAs and make necessary capital provisions in order to meet the eventual loss from those NPAs. As these capital provisions make a dent into the net worth of the bank this will result in erosion of the bank's net worth. This in turn will lead to curtailing the ability of bank to give loans and advances since the quantum of loans and advances of the banks are linked to the bank's net worth.

As per the current regulatory guidelines banks in India have to maintain a minimum capital adequacy of 9%, which

*Ex-Vice President and Branch Head, Bank of Bahrain and Kuwait, Hyderabad.

effectively means that a bank can lend only to the extent of 11.11 times of its networth. Therefore, when there is an erosion of networth due to write off of loans or losses this in turn will result in restriction of lendable funds by a bank. Hence, incidence of NPAs will lead to a chain of negative impacts that will have a multiplier effect to the bank's top line, bottom line and capital and net worth. In view of these factors banks would prefer to avoid NPAs by adopting strategies such as lending only to viable ventures, avoiding risky portfolios. In spite of such careful approach banks still face NPAs since an advance that is considered very good at the time of lending may turn into a bad one due to several factors which may not be under the control of banks.

Broadly the reasons for a unit becoming sick can be attributed to (i) external factors (ii) internal factors. Global market conditions, domestic market conditions, business cycles, government policies are some of the major external factors whereas wrong business strategies, bad planning and execution, HR issues, poor financial planning are some of the major internal factors which cause the sickness of a unit. The immediate reaction of a banker when a unit becomes sick is to identify ways to wriggle out from the relationship by recovering the dues. This knee jerk reaction of banks led to the adage that banker is one who lends an umbrella and snatches it away when it rains heavily !!!. When the bankers see no prospects of a turnaround of the borrower's unit they either make a compromise settlement by waiving a portion of the loan or resort to distress sale of the properties held with them as collaterals to walk out from the relationship. Where the bankers feel that the unit can be turned around by infusing additional funds, they sanction additional credit facilities or through financial restructuring give the required oxygen to the sick unit for revival. However the role of bankers in cases of such revivals is confined to financial support. Only in cases of large advances that have become sick the bank nominates its officials as directors on the board of such sick corporates thereby assuming an additional role of taking active part in management and revival of the sick corporate units. These are the traditional methods so far employed by banks in general in handling the NPAs.

Current Status of NPAs of Banks in India

The non-performing assets of the banking sector increased to 1.28 per cent in 2011-12 from 0.97 per cent in 2010-11 due to slowdown in the economy. According to CRISIL report (August 2012) the portfolio of restructured loans are to the tune of Rs.1.6 Trillion in 2012 and first quarter of 2013 and these loans mostly relate to power, infrastructure and construction activities. During 2012-13 the restructured loan portfolio of Indian banks under CDR (Corporate Debt Restructuring) mechanism is estimated at Rs.71,000 Crs compared to Rs.40,000 Crs in the year 2011-12. The Gross Non-Performing Advances (GNPA) ratio of SCBs (scheduled commercial banks) improved to 3.4 per cent as at end March 2013 against 3.6 per cent as at end September 2012. The net NPA ratio declined to 1.4 per cent as at end March 2013 from 1.6 per cent as at end September 2012. While global factors like recession in US and Europe have led to slow down of Indian economy and affected the performance of several business enterprises, India has added its woes by policy paralysis by govt and bureaucratic hurdles in implementation of several large infrastructure projects.

Delays in implementation of major infrastructure projects has led to Rs,52,445 Crores escalation in their original cost estimates from Rs.1,45,271 Cr to Rs. 1,97,716 Cr as on 31st May 2012.

Breakup:

Category	No of projects	Original cost	Revised estimates	Net increase in cost
Power	28	86,681.80 Cr	99,654.00 Cr	1 2,972.20 Cr
Railways	36	25,089.00 Cr	62,483.00 Cr	37,394.00 Cr
Roads	84	33,500.20 Cr	35,579.00 Cr	2,078.80 Cr
Total	148	1,45,271.00Cr	1,97,716.00Cr	52,445.00 Cr

Source: Deccan Chronicle dated 21st August 2012.

This delay in implementation of large infrastructure projects not only led to cost escalation but also resulted in delays in repayment of dues of many such infrastructure projects funded by banks. In order to avoid these large projects becoming NPAs banks had to resort to restructuring of loans. In accordance with RBI guidelines Indian banks have to maintain a capital adequacy of 9 percent as against 8 percent effective from 1st April 2013 in a phased manner in compliance of the Basel III norms. According to RBI estimates Indian banks would require an additional capital fund of Rs.5 trillion to comply with the Basle III norms over the next five years. Therefore, maintaining quality assets portfolio is very crucial for the banks in India since NPAs will not only reduce the profitability of banks but also lead to erosion of the banks' net worth resulting in falling short of the minimum capital adequacy of 9 percent. Slowdown in economic growth due to global factors and domestic issues is leading India towards recession which has a potential threat to Indian banks in swelling their portfolio of NPAs.

Out of Box Thinking Approach "Successful People don't do different things, they do things differently."—Shiv Khera, Management expert

Banks in fact sit on a hidden treasure but mostly unaware that this could be a very useful resource in turning around the sick borrower accounts. Banks normally have diverse clients spread across various sectors and activities pan India basis and this could very well be of immense use for revival of sick units. A potential list of suppliers and customers for the sick units can be easily identified from the existing customers' data base of the bank. Bank can share this information with the sick units so that these sick units can approach those potential suppliers and customers for business relationship. Bank can as well do a referral to such potential list of suppliers and customers about the possibility of business relationship with sick units. This will add fillip to the revival of the sick units especially when the bank has already infused additional finance or restructured the existing debt with more favourable repayment terms to the beleaguered borrower clients. The cash flows generated through the business relationship established with these potential suppliers and buyers by the sick units is normally routed through the financing banker which ensures effective monitoring of the operations of these sick units. These measures of the bank would enable the sick units to turn around much faster in view of an intégrated approach taken by the bank where the financial package is supported by adding more suppliers and buyers that would not only strengthen the operations but also expand the cash flows of the sick units to bring them on the track of revival.

Strategies for Faster Turnaround

1. **Sharing of the Clients' Data Base:** Sharing of the clients' database among all the banks is very much needed to identify the appropriate suppliers and buyers who would fit into the business plan of the sick units. This can be made possible by accessing the common data base of all the banks currently held with CIBIL. Normally the banks use this database with CIBIL to do verification of the banking transaction history of clients/prospective clients while giving credit facilities. Banks can share the detailed profile of their clients highlighting their nature of business in addition to the banking arrangements with CIBIL so that CIBIL will maintain the detailed profiles of banks 'clients. Since all banks have access to this CIBIL's data base, generating the list of prospective suppliers and buyers for sick units would be a much easier task.
2. **Referral of Prospective Suppliers and Buyers;** On a careful evaluation of the sick units the bank can suitably identify the right target segment of prospective suppliers and buyers from the detailed profile of banks 'clients to be maintained with CIBIL as suggested above. Bank can do a referral to both

the prospective suppliers and buyers as well as to the sick units in order to bring them together in their mutual business interests.

3. **Integrated Financial Restructuring:** Infusion of additional finance or restructuring the existing debt with more favorable terms like extension of the loan tenor, reduction in the amount of loan installments, lowering the interest rates,etc should be decided by the bank only after due consideration of the steps 1 and 2 mentioned above. This will lead to an effective restructuring plan by integration of the financial plans with business plans proposed for the rehabilitation of sick units.

4. **Flexible Funding Mechanism:** In order to make the above mentioned business plan achievable, the funding pattern proposed under financial restructuring should be suitably modified with greater flexibility in operations. In other words, banks should look for an ideal combination of both funded and non funded limits to constitute an effective overall financial package. Banks to issue letters of credit and or bank guarantees to enable the sick units to procure the required raw materials/stocks from the suppliers. Receivable finance and bill discounting facilities are to be provided by the banks to the sick units for their credit sales. To ensure proper financial discipline for the sick units, from the proceeds of receivable finance and bill discounting a portion of funds can be impounded by the banks towards recoveries, of over dues. This type of structuring of the credit facilities would provide flexibility in operations to the sick units and also ensure a smooth flow of recovery of debts by the banks from the cash flows of the unit without pinching the borrower too much. This mechanism would lead to recoveries of the debts by the bank in proportion to the cash flows of the sick units without affecting the routine operations which is justifiable.

Issues

Human Resources and Expertise

Most of the banks do not possess adequate human resources as well as expertise to handle the NPAs and design effective turn around strategies for sick units. Added to this there are various layers and hierarchies in the organizations (i.e., banks) that only lead to delays and communication gaps resulting in sealing the fate of sick units rather than giving them the financial life support systems to bring them on track. While proper financial support is important in the case of revival of sick units, timely financial support is very crucial since the patient is already in ICU !!. Therefore the above mentioned constraints faced by the banks only result in adding more patients in ICU after making them seriously ill rather than giving proper preventive care while they are in OP category or in general ward. This is one of the basic causes which accelerate the pace of sickness of business units. Very few banks have the required human resources and expertise to handle this situation. The number of banks who handle the sick units on a fast track is also very limited. A lot more is required to be done in this area in Indian banking industry and this is possible only by drafting suitable HR policies to develop the expertise and by setting up a lean hierarchy to ensure faster decision making in revival and rehabilitation of sick units.

An integrated approach towards management of NPAs by banks as suggested above would add to the value chain in addition to infusing the much needed funds to propel momentum to the working capital cycle and facilitate smooth cash flows for operations of sick borrowers to turn around.

Case Study

ABC Industries Ltd (ABCIL) is engaged in manu-facturing cold rolled steel. ABCIL went for expansion of production capacity through acquisition of another company. Unfortunately the company's expansion plans hit a tumbling block due to recession in the economy which had severely impacted the steel industry. This led to sharp decline in the sales turnover of the company by 80 percent and huge operating losses. ABCIL was not able to repay its debts and service the interest payments to its bankers due to heavy losses. ABCIL approached the bankers for CDR package. ABCIL prepared its revival plan focusing on (i) business restructuring by adding new products like manufacturing components to auto and white goods sectors, tube products, railway coach profiles etc as a part of diversification and de-risking strategy, (ii) Improvement of productivity by energy savings, rationalization of work force post-acquisition, efficient management of inventories and receivables leading to better working capital management.

Bankers were convinced with the company's revival plan and implemented CDR package wherein the long term debt was rescheduled with longer tenor, interest rates were reduced which resulted in improving the liquidity position of the company to tiave a smooth working capital cycle. **Additionally the bankers took the initiative to refer new clients to ABCIL in the segments like-automobiles and white goods. This initiative of the bankers has improved the order book position of ABCIL.** In view of its improved order book position ABCIL came forward to repay its bankers an extra sum of 10 percent of its turnover from realization of its sales receivables over and above as per the rescheduled terms. The above measures collectively have resulted in ABCIL coming on the path of recovery and growth one year ahead of the schedule. While the company's revival strategy was implemented with company's commitment and supported by suitable CDR package of the banks, referring new clients by banks to ABCIL has added further boost to turnaround strategy and enabled the bankers to recover their dues one year ahead of schedule as per the CDR plan.

Conclusion

Slow down of Indian economy due to policy paralysis and the impact of global recession is posing greater challenges to

Indian banks in managing the NPAs. Basel III norms that require banks to maintain higher capital adequacy of 9% as against 8% hitherto would be adding fuel to the fire. Therefore a paradigm shift is needed in the approach of banks towards NPA management. In this paper the author has suggested few simple yet effective strategies to be adopted by banks which will strengthen the network of suppliers and customers of sick companies leading to better cash flows and smooth working capital cycle. The author has highlighted the need for an integrated financial restructuring with a flexible funding mechanism to supplement the above strategies. In support of his views the author has substantiated the points from a case study analysis.

Key words

- CDR - Corporate Debt Restructuring - is an institutional mechanism evolved by RBI for implementation by financial institutions and banks to restructure the debts of troubled corporate clients.
- BASEL III NORMS - These are the guidelines laid down by Bank for international settlements to improve the regulation, supervision and risk management within the banking sector across the world.
- CIBIL - Credit Information Bureau (India) Limited - This institution collects and maintains the records pertaining to the payments of loans and credit cards of individuals and commercial entities in India.
- FUNDED AND NON-FUNDED LIMITS - funded limits are those given by banks and financial institutions where it involves outlay of funds. Non-funded limits are given by banks and financial institutions that primarily do not involve outlay of funds but enables the borrowers of banks to procure materials on credit from suppliers (e.g. Letters of credit) or obtain work orders/contracts from clients where the

performance obligation of the borrowers is guaranteed by the banks (e.g.- bank guarantee)

- RECEIVABLE FINANCE - Financing against the sales invoices to the seller of goods by the banks and FIs where the final payment by the buyer of goods is made on a later date.
- BILL DISCOUNTING - Financing against the sales bills to the seller of goods by the banks and FIs backed by the purchaser's acceptance of hundi/bill of exchange to make the final payment on a later date.

REFERENCES

CRISIL REPORT (August 2012).

Financial stability report, June 2013, by Reserve Bank of India.

Deccan Chronicle dated 21st August 2012.

11

E-banking Products and Its Acceptance
A Special Focus on Internet Banking in Indian Scenario

—K. Srinivasa Rao*

—Dr. R.N. Misra**

The Indian banking industry is governed by the Banking Regulation Act of India, 1949 and functioning under the regulatory and supervisory guidelines of the Reserve Bank of India (RBI). During 1980s, the RBI started banking modernization exercises with the introduction of new technology in telecommunication through Internet which are cost effective, reliable and fast. ATM, RTGS, NEFT, MICR, ECS, CTS and Internet Banking are the some of the innovative e-Banking Products introduced by the Indian banks with the support of new technology.

It is seen that about 75% of Public sector bank operations are fully internet enabled as on march 2012 (RBI, 2012). Out of these nearly 90% PSB branches are running under core banking solutions. In spite of being the group with the largest number of branches spread all over this vast country, State Bank Group has already fully computerized 99.9 percent of its branches. 95 per cent of the State Bank group branches are presently running on CBS and few of its associates have all their branches under Core Banking Services.

Online banking facilities offered by various financial institutions have many features and capabilities in common, but also have some that are application specific. Even though

*Lecturer in Commerce, Government College, Razole, E.G. Distt.

**Retired Professor in Commerce, Gandhi Nagar, Berhampur-760001

entire world accession the internet banking, Indian internet banking system is lagging behind of its some barriers. The present study **"E-banking Products and Its Acceptance —A Special Focus On Internet Banking In Indian Scenario"** deals with the Present Internet banking facilities available in India and its acceptance from the customer side. Pros and cons of the internet banking in Indian scenario.

Electronic banking is defined as the automated delivery of banking products and services directly to customers through electronic, interactive communication channels.

E-banking includes the systems that enable financial institution customers, individuals or businesses, to access accounts, transact business, or obtain information on financial products and services through a public or private network, including the internet.

Modern e-banking first appeared in New York in the early 1980's, which was offered by Citibank and Chase Manhattan. The United Kingdom banks started to adopt the concept in 1983 where the Bank of Scotland was the first to introduce it.

In India, ICICI bank was the first bank which offered this delivery channel and online services in 1996. Other private sector banks like Citibank, Induslnd Bank and HDFC and Times bank (now part of HDFC bank) started offering internet services in 1999. State bank of India launched its services in July 2001 and the other SCB's so on.

The term e-banking consists in the forms of Virtual banking, on-line banking, cyber-banking, net-banking, interactive-banking, web-banking, phone-banking, PC-banking, and remote electronic banking. The familiar e-Banking products are ATM, RTGS, NEFT, MICR, ECS, CTS etc.

Services Provided by Net Banking

- Transfer funds between individual accounts
- Transfer funds to a third party Transactions

- Ask for a Account Statements
- Check Balance
- Pay Bills
- Shop Online
- Pay Bank Credit Card Dues
- Ask for a Demand Draft
- Stop a Cheque request
- Request for a new Fixed deposit and payment

Internet-Banking in Indian Scenario

According to *Economic Survey 2011-12*, in total 98% of public sector bank branches have been fully computerized.

Currently, India has 88 scheduled commercial banks (SCBs) - 26 public sector banks and 21 private banks and 36 foreign banks. They have a combined network of over 53,000 branches and 17,000 ATMs.

The current statistics show that hardly 10 per cent of Indian customers uses the internet for banking. Among all the facilities provided, the maximum of them uses only for checking balance. Very few customers use the advance interactive services provided by the banks.

According to HDFC and ICICI Bank, 17 per cent of ICICI customers use the Internet for banking and 10 per cent of HDFC customers prefer it.

Top 5 Countries with the Highest Number of Internt Users

Sl.No.	Country	Internet Users (Latest)	Penetration % of Population	World %Users
1.	China	513100000	38.4%	22.5%
2.	USA	245203319	78.3%	10.8%
3.	India	121000000	10.2%	5.3%
4.	Japan	101228736	80.0%	4.4%
5.	Brazil	81798000	42.2%	3.6%

Source: *Indian Journal of Research.*

Objectives of the Study

1. to identify the usage of internet banking among the customers
2. to identify the factors that were influencing internet banking adoption among customers in India.
3. to analyze Customer perception on Internet Banking.
4. to identify the main obstacles for adoption of electronic banking.

Methodology of the Study

This paper is based on secondary data collected from websites of various banks to analyse the usage of e-banking products. Primary data collected from 100 sample units consisting of Bank Customers with a qualification of below graduate level, graduate level, Post Graduate level, Business People and Bankers. This sample units were selected under convenient sampling technique and structurequestioner was posted. The responses from respondents were analyzed in a systernatic manner and statistical tools like Correlation, Likert Scale, ANOVA, were used.

Analysis of Data

The respondents comprised of 40 (40%) Under Graduates, 20(20%) Graduates, 10 (10%)Post Graduates,10(10%) Business People and 10(10%) Bank officials.

1. Among the below graduate respondents, there is a low internet banking operation due to non accessible to computer and lack of internet facility and awareness of e-Banklng.
2. More than 75% of the respondents from Graduate. Post-Graduate Customers and Business people revealed that they were feeling Comfortable with internet banking. The remaining were felt somewhat uncomfortable due to technological and security barriers.

3. There is a positive correlation to the Computer literacy and e-Banking usage.
4. From Banking personals perception e-banklng facility is cost benefit and time saving. The main enabler of internet banking is "convenience" or "24×7 accessibility".
5. It is observed that some of the first generation bank employees have not access to the e-banking products.

Conclusion

Based on the findings of this study the following suggestions could be arrived at:

1. Banks could facilitate internet banking to the customers as easier to use.
2. Banks have to adopt the policy of creating awareness among the customers about e-banking facilities.
3. Banks should ensure that online banking is safe and secure for financial transaction like traditional banking.
4. Banks should organize seminar and conference to educate the customer regarding uses of online banking as well as security and privacy of their accounts.
5. Some customers are hindered by lack of access to online banking. They should be provided online banking facilities in the banks.

12

Digital Banking
A Revolution in Financial Deals

—Prof. R.P. Sarma*

Economic system is changing fast in recent year after revolutionary introduction of electronic devices in day-to-day activities of the social system. Economy now reached to 4-G stage. In the ancient primitive economy was called Forest Economy which is termed as 1-G economy. Next economy, the Agricultural Economy remained for centuries which have known as 2-G economy. With the developmenl of industries and industrial revolution the economic system changed considerably from the early 19th century until the end of 20th century which can be termed as 3-G economy. Now from the beginning of the twenty-first century the electronic media entered into every walk of life and makes the life more comfortable to live in the world than ever before. This is now known as Digital Economy, the Fourth Generation Economy or 4-G economy. All transaction of government and social business is now performed on-line for quick and efficient purpose. The activities of government are now being switched on progressively on digital basis.

What is Digital Banking?

Now a bank customer need not go to a bank office to make any transaction in the bank; by sitting at home or office or

*Director, Institute of Economic Studies, Jayaprakash Nagar, Brahmapur-760010.

while traveling or sitting in a park, at any time of the day or night, can do all the banking transactions without any difficulty. Only requirement is a digital devise of Inter-net. A bank customer can perform all these transaction usually done by him by going to a bank building and / also many more.

- Viewing account balances,
- Viewing recent transactions,
- Downloading of bank statements in PDF format,
- Viewing; the images of paid cheques,
- Ordering cheque books,
- Periodic account statements,
- Funds transfer from customers linked accounts,
- Payment to third party bills,
- Investment purchase or sale,
- Loan applications and all transaction in this regard.

If all the banking transactions can be performed sitting at home there is no necessity of a person to visit a bank office. A. Digital Bank not only saves time and cost of travel to a bank, but transactions of national and international financial deals are at the flick of a second; now it is being visualized to evolve an international monitor) unit common to all the nations for all type of international financial deals. It is hoped that day is not far away as the world is moving at this rate.

First Initiative

The Digital Banking, known first as "on-line banking" as there was no set identity for it earlier, first introduced in New York City in early 1980s. Four major banks of the city, Citibank, Chase Manhattan, Chemical and Manufacturers Hanover. Chemical introduced its "Pronto Service" for individuals and small businesses in 1983, The customers are allowed to maintain *Electronic Cheque Book* registers and can see account balances, transfer of funds and maintain saving accounts. But Pronto failed to attract enough customers and the experiment was abandoned in 1989. By 2000, 80 percent of US banks offered e-banking. A significant cultural change took place after the Y2K scare ended. In 2001 Bank of America become the first bank to top 3 million on line banking customers.

In U.K. the first on line banking service known as Homelink was setup by Bank of Scotland for the customers of the Nottingham Building Society (NBS), in 1983. The system used was based on the UK's Prestel Viewlink system and used a computer, such as BBC Micro connected to telephone system and television set. The system allowed on-line viewing of statements, bank transfers and bill payments. Stanford Federal Credit Union was the first financial institution to offer on-line internet banking service to all its members in October 1994. In 2009 it was reported by Gartner Group estimate that 47 percent of US adults and 30 percent of UK people bank through online.

Britons are using Internet and mobiles for financial transactions worth nearly 1 billion pounds a day and branch use is falling sharply. In response, banks are expected to close more unprofitable branches while they invest in mobile and online services for customers. Internet and mobile banking is now used for transactions worth 6.4 billion pounds a week in Britain, up from 5.8 billion last year. Royal Bank of Scotland said last month it was inevitable that it would close more of its 1,900 branches after branch transactions fell by 30 percent over the past 3 years.

Barclays, Lloyds and HSBC are also expected to close branches, according to industry sources. The Campaign for Community Banking Services, a lobby group, has warned that further closures could have a damaging impact on rural communities that rely on local branches for banking services and called for measures such as brandi sharing to avoid the last branches left in a particular area being shut down. But the BBA said branches would remain integral to banking in the 21st century. It said 2,274 bank branches had been refurbished in the past two years, underlining banks' commitment to their high street outlets. "Day-to-day branch use is falling sharply and while the size of these networks will decline, high street outlets will remain important for those bigger moments, such as when a customer takes out a mortgage, wants to assess their financial options or resolve a complaint.

Bank analysis reports show that over the next five years more than two-thirds of banking customers are likely to be "self-directed" and highly adapted to the online world. In fact, these same consumers already act much more digitally in other industries - booking flights and holidays, buying hooks and music, and increasingly shopping for groceries and other goods via digital channels. Once a credible digital banking proposition exists customer adoption will be breathtakingly fast and digital laggards will be left exposed.

It is estimated that digital transformation will put upwards of 30 per cent of the revenues of a typical bank in play, particularly in the high turnover, less sticky products like personal loans and payments. We also estimate that banks can take out 20 to 25 per cent of their cost base by leveraging this digital shift to transform how they process and service. Put together, the economics of a digital bank will give it a vast competitive edge over a traditional incumbent. It's therefore fair to say that getting digital banking right is a case of do-or-die.

The Third Wave

The first wave on-line banking was initiated in the 1980s with limited success, later in 2000-10 the second wave of changes came with the fast changing internet system of WWW with a small success, but now the Third Wave of Digital System with its more sophisticated electronic devices will sweep the traditional banking system for good. Technological advances make the third wave of digital banks look more sustainable. The proliferation and sophistication of smart phones and tablets allow banks to offer many more services online. Instead of having to choose between queuing in a branch or sitting down in front of a computer, customers can now check balances or pay bills using their phones while sitting on the bus. They can deposit cheques by photographing them and accept credit-card payments using their phones. As a result, the number of transactions taking place in branches is falling steadily.

Customer Preference

The recent developments in digital devices led to attracting digital Banking system more and more:

1. Improvements in user-experience design through interactive, game-like interfaces that are starting to merge tire boundaries between the real and the virtual and bringing data to life through rich visualisations.
2. Advances in mobile devices and networks., providing new services such as enhanced digital security and the ability to access the Internet from anywhere.
3. The rise of social media and collaboration tools, empowering customers and employees, and moving control of the 'brand message" from businesses to consumers.
4. Innovation in digital analytics and predictive models, driving deeper insight into customers' behaviour and enabling highly targeted and relevant treatment strategies to be executed through digital media.
5. New channel integration technologies, enabling a more seamless end-to-end experience lor customers with their bank.

The bank customers now prefer more to Digital Banks than the traditional Building Banks.

Present-day consumers expect high quality digital communication. Rich content including elegant designs, instant search results and interactive features. Bank websites, especially online banking sections, are now required to offer a pleasant experience while remaining highly functional. It is still common for banks to send out account statements using the postal service: however, for many people digital banking offers 24/7 account balance control - there is a clear preference, especially for younger customers, to want instantaneous access to their accounts. The posted account statement is snail mail in comparison.

Consumers have access to more information then ever before, they now communicate with more people and more frequently - traditional word-of-mouth has a completely different meaning when one considers the immediacy of Facebook, Twitter or even email. Access to information and the ease with which consumers can share views with those they know is dramatic. Good experiences can be easily shared online. It is important that banks understand the importance of customer thinking in deciding where to trust their money and in choosing their primary banking relationship.

Banks should consider four main aspects of a robust digital offering:

1. Customer attitudes and behaviour are changing
2. Digital is preferred globally
3. Digital is a part of Generation Y's lifestyle and this is the key time for them to decide on their primar banking relationship.
4. Digital is evolving — technology devices and software all serve to disrupt traditional means of communication. Simultaneously, each brings opportunity.

Manual Dealings are Declining

It is found that the direct hand-to-hand bank transaction is no sharp declning trend. The average number cashier transactions per branch have sharply declined per month. In US per branch monthly cash transaction sharply came down from $7.5 thousand to $ 6.0 thousand from the year 2008 to 2012.

Fig. 12.1 indicates the declining trend of cash transactions in recent years graphically.

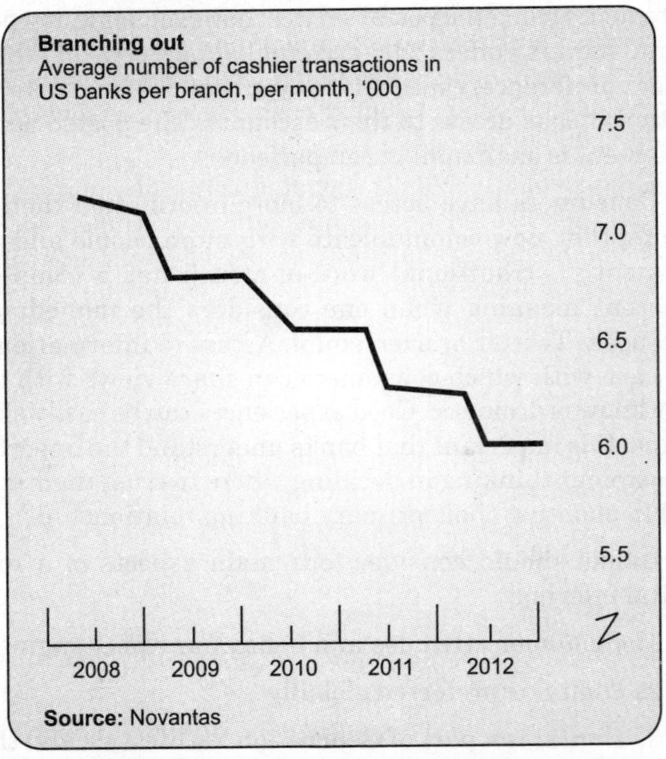

Digital Bank is Easier

Joining online banks is much easier these days. In markets where regulators allow it. Hello lets customers open new accounts entirely online, using smart phones to take photographs of their identity documents and utility bills. New online banks are also able to offer customers things the old ones couldn't. For example, Simple has a clever search box that enables customers to type in queries such as "How much did I spend on taxis in New York last month?" or "How much have I spent on coffee this week?" Holvi has built its bank around an accounting system that lets groups of friends or workers at small firms manage budgets and allocate funds to projects.

Reducing the number of branches offers the potential for huge savings, since these accounts for about half of all costs in retail banking. Yet the dilemma facing banks, new and old, is that the most complex and profitable financial products, such as mortgages, are still sold in branches. It also tends to be easier to entire customers to use several such, products in person.

Britons are using Internet and mobile banking for transactions worth nearly one billion pounds a day and branch use is falling sharply. In response, banks are expected to close more unprofitable branches while they invest in mobile and online services for customers who want to bank while on the move. Internet and mobile banking is now used for transactions worth 6.4 billion pounds a week in Britain, up from 5.8 billion last year, the report showed. Banking apps for mobile devices have been downloaded more than 14.7 million times - up 2.3 million just since January - while Internet banking services are typically receiving 7 million log-ins each day.

Closing of Physical Branches!

Royal Bank of Scotland said that it was inevitable that it would close more of its 1900 branches after branch transactions fell by 30 percent over the past three years. Barclays, Lloyds and HSBC are also expected to close branches. The Campaign for Community Banking Services, a lobby group, has warned that further closures could have a damaging impact on rural communities that rely on local tranches for banking services and called for measures such as branch sharing to avoid the last branches left in a particular area being shut down.

But the BBA said branches would remain integral to banking in the 21st century. It said 2274 bank branches, had been refurbished in the past two years, underlining banks' commitment to their high street outlets. Day-to-day branch use is falling sharply and while the size of these networks will decline, high street outlets will remain important for those bigger moments, such as when a customer takes out a mortgage, wants to assess their financial options or resolve a complaint. Banks arc looking to automate more basic banking services within branches, such as withdrawing and depositing cash and paying bills, freeing up staff to focus on offering advice. But Paul Adams, chief executive of Glory Global Solutions, which provides self-service machines for bank branches, said British lenders have yet to fully grasp the opportunity provided by new technology to improve customer experiences. RBS said last month that over 400 of its branches across Britain would be fitted with new technology including iPads so that customers can register and access online banking. Industry sources say a surge in the popularity of mobile banking applications is the main driver behind the rise in digital transactions. The growth in mobile transactions has been "phenomenal" over the past two years.

The Asian Scene

Asia's banks trail the rest of the world when it comes to digital banking. The slower embrace of online banking comes even as the region's increasingly affluent consumer base is tipped to drive demand for internet products linked to savings, credit cards and loans. Mobile and internet banking across Asia has jumped 35 percent in the past three years while visits to branches have dropped by 27 percent in the same period. For some lenders, the rush by consumers to manage their finances on the internet is viewed as a threat. In China, internet firms such as Alibaba and Tencent have irked big lenders by offering products traditionally sold by state banks including mobile payment services and online investment products.

Almost two billion digital banking consumers could be based in Asia by 2020, led by China, India and South East Asia. In China alone the number of digital consumers is expected to surge to 900 million in 2020 from 380 million in 2012.

Voice Banking ?

In a Singapore laboratory, one of the world's biggest lenders is working on a system at the frontier of digital banking; voice recognition. Citigroup Inc., whose retail branches span the globe, is developing technology that will allow customers using telephone banking to be recognized by their voice, bypassing the need for repeating passwords or personal identification numbers and cutting the required time to green light transactions. Trials have been conducted in Malaysia and Singapore ahead of a planned roll out by year end.

Citi isn't the first bank to experiment with voice biometrics and the technology has been around for decades. Others, such as Barclays and Wells Fargo are also developing programs. National Australia Bank embraced biometrics as far back as 2012. U.S. based Nuance Communications Inc. have developed voice technology that can be used in banking. The voice automation process is likely years away from being used on ATMs, for example. Questions also remain about its reliability and effectiveness and banking executives say the technology is expensive.

Cyber Crime

Cyber crime remains a key threat in Digital Banking. China alone lost $46 billion through cyber crime in 2012, 40 percent of total global losses, according to Symantec. Around 95 percent of Citi's customer transactions in Asia now happen outside branches, while around half of its 16 million customers in the region bank online. As part of its online push, the U.S. lender has remodeled its retail stores across the region to resemble Apple outlets. It used the same design firm, 8 Inc., to overhaul its branches. Instead of a traditional scene of bank clerks and scattered paper chits, customers are met by sleekly designed outlets complete with iPads, wireless internet and hardly a scrap of paper lo be seen.

The Initiative in India

India has to wail for a full-fledged digital Banking until July 2014, even though internet-banking on a small scale is being working in several banks. The State Bank of India in July 2014 launched six digital branches across the country as part of its programme to offer next generation banking services. These branches, named SBI-INTOUCH, will facilitate services such as instant account opening with personalised debit cards, instant loan approval for car and home, remote expert advisors available via video links. Besides Delhi, where SBI-INTOUCH branch was inaugurated by Finance Minister Arun Jaitley, the other such branches are located in Mumbai, Bangalore, Chennai and Ahmedabad.

In inaugural address Mr. Jetly hoped that with the innovative technology and user-friendly features at the digital stores, SBI has led the way in digital innovation in the Indian banking industry. Digital banking is making an honorable entry into India, The mergence of new. technologies and expectations of tech-sawy customers is changing the way banking is conducted in the country. Indian banks are also proving that they are riot behind their global counterparts. Traditional banking involved several visits to your nearest bank branch and wasting hours, but that's a thing of the past with India, where 50 per cent of population is yet to experience banking services, now flirting with digital banking.

The SBI says digital stores will be bringing several unique and different offers to the new-age customers. These will include, for the first time in India, instant issuance of personalized debit cards created through an instant account opening kiosk, instant in-principle loan approval and an interactive dream wall to aid customers in conceptualizing their journey towards realizing their financial dreams.

Conclusions

The banking system operating in the villages with the money lender from ancient days was institutionalised from 19th century, but to-day with the advent of electronic revolution changed the concept of banking. One cannot imagine that the future banking operation would run without cash, cheque or drafts without any paper in simply accounts and numbers over the globe perhaps ignoring the units of money of the nations and accepting what would be called Global Money or GM.

13

Innovative Banking for Financial Inclusion *A Study*

—Dr. Prafulla Chandra Mohanty*

Introduction

In a developing country, the banking sector has played a multi-dimensional and multi-directional role in overall development. In India the role of banking has changed significantly over the period since Independence. The period can broadly be divided in three phases such as the period before nationalization (1947-1969), period before liberalization (1969-1991) and the period after liberalization since 1991 to till now onwards. During these periods Indian banking got a momentum in poverty alleviation, improving rural and financial infrastructure, in diminishing the breadth of financial exclusion and so targeting at reaching the hundred percent financial inclusions.

There have been many positive developments in the Indian banking sector during the past decades. Changes in policy and regulations brought about during this period have led to an overall improvement in the growth, asset, quality and profitability of our banks; so that they now compare very favourably with other banks in the region.

Banking index has grown at a compounded annual rate of 51 percent since April 2001 as compared to a 27 percent

*Principal (Retd.). Sankurti Sadan, Kutcheri Ghar village Boyali Po: Mantridi Distt: Ganjam, Odisha.

growth in the market index during this period. The capital to risk weighted assets ratio (CRAR) for all the scheduled commercial banks has increased to 13.2 percent from 11.4 percent in 2001, which is more than the eight percent requirement specified under Basel frameworks, or the percent norm adopted by the RBI for an Indian Bank.

Outstanding records of the growth and innovation have been established by same banks. Even the public sector banks stood up have to the challenge posed by the new private banks, and has worked consciously upon improving their efficiency. The fact that Indian banks have come out almost unscathed through the global down turn in a year that has such the fall of several leading banks, speaks volumes about their resilience.

Bank penetration continues to be rather low in the country, despite expansion of services in rural areas. Financial inclusion holds top priority for policy-makers today, because unless we are able to meet the credit needs of our people, we can never hope to grow in a sustainable way. In order to reach the maximum number of people in the most efficient manner, banks need to have robust risk management practices, advanced technology, skilled man power and very sound marketing practices. All this would require huge investment, the capacity to face challenges and competitions from foreign banks. With innovations in products and services coming up every day, banks also need to acquire new skills, marketing and credit operations.

Globally speaking, the segments that have not been brought in to the fold of the basic banking services are said to be financial excluded. Financial exclusion is the lack of access by certain consumers to appropriate, low cost, fair and safe financial products and services from mainstream providers. There is a large overlap between poverty and permanent financial exclusion. Both poverty and financial exclusion result in a reduction of choices of which affects of social interaction and leads to reduces participation in the society, thus leading to social exclusion. Bringing all these people into the fold of banking services is "financial inclusion". Thus financial inclusion is delivery of banking services at an affordable cost to the vast sections of disadvantaged and low income groups.

Financial inclusion can be thought of in two ways. One is exclusion from the payments system i.e. having access to a bank account. The second type of exclusion is from formal credit markets, requiring the excluded to approach informal and exploitative markets. After nationalization of major banks in India in 1969, there was a significant expansion of branch network to unbanked areas and stepping up of lending to agriculture small industry and business. More recently, the focus is on establishing the right of every person to have access to affordable basic banking services. The financial excluded sections largely comprise marginal farmers, landless labours, oral lessees, self-employed and unorganized sector enterprises, urban slum dwellers, migrants, etc. mostly the illiterates are largely found in the stream. The extent of financial exclusion in the country would leave us stunned. Some of the few areas are of inclusion are insurance up to ten percent, in again purchasing health products of same insurance is 0.20 percent and incase of receiving entrepreneurial credit to the beneficiary is only 3.65 percent.

Objectives, Methodology and Scope of the Study

With this backdrop, the paper deals with the conceptual parts of innovative banking services rendered for financial inclusion, the reasons of exclusion, the need, strategies, various steps to be taken for increasing the number inclusion. Towards the end the chapter gives a author view on the future of financial inclusion and its dependence for economic development. The study arrived through simple mathematical and statistical tools. Mostly the data collected from secondary sources for preparation and analysis. Scope of financial inclusion can be expanded in two ways such as:

(*a*) Through state driven intervention by a ways of statutory enactments.

(*b*) Through voluntary effort by the banking community it self for evolving various strategies to bring within the orbit of the banking sector the large strata of society.

Financial Inclusion

The financial excluded are the persons who have remained out of the financial track. But the financial inclusion make the person to get all the advantages of financial system and the services. The consequences of financial exclusion will vary depending on the nature and extent of services denied, it may lead to higher incidence of crime, general decline in investment, difficulties in gaining access to credit or getting credit from in formal sources at exorbitant rates and increased unemployment, etc. The small business may suffer due to loss of access to middle class and higher income consumers, higher case handling costs, delays in remittances of money. Some of the steps are given to attract the small man for financial inclusion. Such as:

- Huge branches of commercial, co-operative regional rural and other kinds of banks to be opened.
- Focus on credit rather than other services like savings, insurances etc.
- Landing to priority sectors like to agriculture, weaker sections of the population, etc.
- Interest ceilings significant government subsidies channeled through the banks and cooperatives as a government programs.
- Financing poor as a social obligation but not as a potential business or commercial opportunity.

There are various reasons for financial exclusion. In remote, hilly and scarcely populated areas with poor infrastructure, physical access it self acts as a deterrent. Lack of awareness, low incomes, are the causes of social exclusion.

Illiteracy acts as barriers for financial inclusion. Distance from the branch, the stipulated timings, cumbersome documentation and procedures, unsuitable products, language, staff attitudes are the common reason of exclusion. It also makes it difficult to arrange the independent documentary prove of identity and address for transacting through a bank account especially for a poor migrants and slum dwellers. The most needed services for exclusion are accesses to small loans are over draft, Check-in-account, Small savings products, Health insurance products, insurance against the failure of activity financial asset, credit card, entrepreneurship credit.

Strategies to Approach Hundred percent Financial Inclusion

Generally the banks to get 10 percent financial inclusion adopt the following strategies. At the regional level, a forum called the State level bankers committee (SLBC) for 100 percent financial inclusion. The process is successful in Puduchery, Haryana, H.P., Karnataka, Kerala, and Punjab. Reserve Banks propose to undertake an evaluation of the progress made in these regions by an independent external agency to draw lessons for further action in this regard. In the districts taken up for 100 percent financial inclusion, surveys were conducted using various database such as electoral rolls, public distribution system, or other household data, to identify households without bank account and responsibility given to the banks in the area for ensuring that all those who wanted to have a bank Accounts were provided with one by allocating the villages to the different banks.

Mass media was deployed for creating awareness and publicity. The banks used different approaches to communicate the advantages of having a bank account through their staff, their agents who are local NGOs or village volunteers would contact the people at their vicinity. Ration card/ Sectoral ID cards of the families were taken for fulfilling the simplified KYC norms. Photographs of all the persons who opened bank accounts were taken on the spot by a photographer accompanying the bank team.

In most States, the product used for launching the program for financial inclusion is the “no frills accounts”. In one state the farmer’s credit card or KCC (Kishan Credit Card) is being used ensuring first to credit rather than savings. In some states the “no frill” account was followed by small overdraft facility or credit up to a pre-specified limit. Recognizing the need of providing social security to vulnerable groups, in some cases in association with insurance companies, banks have provided innovative insurance policies at affordable cost covering life, disabilities and health cover. Co-operative and regional rural banks being local level institutions are well suited for achieving financial inclusion.

India post is also looking to diversify its activities and leverage on its huge network of post offices, the postman’s intimate knowledge of the local population and the enormous trust reposed in him. Bankers are entering into the agreements with India post for using post offices as agents for branchless banking.

LIC is India’s largest financial institution and has been closely associated with the evaluation and development of the Indian economy reaching to the common class poor through the social security, investment, and credit facility system of financial inclusion.

The Reserve Bank of India has granted in-principle approval that will allow private sector players to promote small local banks in what is seen as a new version of the local area bank (LAB) schemes, withdrawn earlier. These banks will have an area of operations up to three contiguous districts. The proposal came from the Raghuram Rajan Committee appointed by the Planning Commission in its reports in 2008 to insure inclusive banking. These banks are more effective in reaching out to power households, local small enterprises and will help in bridging the gap in credit availability. Local area banks are allowed in under banked or unbanked areas. As of now, the country has as many as one hundred twenty revenue blocks, with no banks facilities.

Some amongst these banks that arrange to establish good track record and wish to raise their own deposits would choose to become small finance banks with a capital base below rupees three hundred crores. Some of these local area banks can at a later stage be allowed to index their operations and raise their stature to become commercial banks, if at all capable in the future.

Number of Saving Accounts to Adult Population

Measuring financial exclusion: one common measure financial inclusion is the percentage of the adult population having bank accounts. Going by available data of the number of savings bank accounts and assuming that one person has only one account (the assumption may not be correct as many persons could have more than one account). We find that in an all India basis, 59 percent of adult populations of the country have bank accounts. In other words, 41 percent of the population of the country is still unbanked. The unbanked population is higher in the north eastern and eastern regions.

The extent of exclusion from credit markets is much more, as number of loan accounts constituted only 14 percent of adult population (tally) in rural areas; the coverage is 9.5 percent against four percent in urban areas. Regional differences are significant with the credit coverage at 25 percent for the southern region and as low as (7.00 percent, 8.2 percent and 9.00 percent respectively in North Eastern, Eastern and Central regions. The extent of exclusion for credit markets can be observed from a different view point. Out of 203 millions households in the country, 147 million are in rural areas, 89 millions are farmer households. 51.4 percent of households have no access to formal or informal sources of credit. Looking at the different sources of credit, it is observed that the share of non-institutional sources reduced from 70.8 percent in 1971 to 42.9 percent in 2002. However after 1991, the share of non-institutional sources has increased; specifically, the share of money-lenders in debt of rural households increased from 17.5 percent in 1991 to 29.6 percent in 2002. In urban areas the share of non-institutional sources has come down significantly from 40 percent in 1981 to around 25 percent in 2002.

Financially Excluded Population

The financially excluded sections largely comprise of marginal farmers, landless labourers, oral lessees self-employed and unorganized sector enterprises, urban shown dwellers, migrants, ethnic minorities and socially excluded group, senior citizens and women. The extent of financial exclusion in the country would leave us stunned. Coverage of survey 10 percent, health insurance 0.20 percent, entrepreneurial credit 3.65 percent. More alarming is that only 5 percent villages are having a bank branch. Out of 400 million poor, SHGs have managed to cover only 125 million poor. Out of 203 million households in the country, 147 million are in rural areas 89 million are farmer household. 51.4 percent of farm households have no access to formal or informal source of credit. 70 percent of marginal landless farmers do not have a bank account and 87 percent have no access to credit from formal sector.

Challenges: The challenges are of structural, social and regulatory. For financial inclusion.

Structural challenges: The structural challenge are the branch expansion in rural unbanked areas. Human resource operation in remote area is not profitable for bank that is nearly adjusting 600 million new customers. Offering a simple load product without proper security is the risk for bank management. Processing capacity of the banks is also limited. To overcome this some central processing centers are required to open.

Statewise Financially Excluded Population
(Percent of farmers in the concerned States who are financially excluded)

Sl. No.	Number of States	Percentage of Exclusion
1	2	3
1.	Tamil Nadu	67.7
2.	Bihar	61.1
3.	Chhattisgarh	58.1
4.	Madhya Pradesh	54.0
5.	Jharkhand	50.3
6.	Rajasthan	49.7
7.	Karnataka	49.6
8.	West Bengal	48.2
9.	Uttar Pradesh	45.4
10.	Odisha	42.2
11.	Gujarat	37.3
12.	Haryana	36.3
13.	Assam	31.2
14.	Andhra Pradesh	24.6
15.	North Eastern States	22.7
16.	Maharashtra and Goa	21.2
17.	Punjab and Chandigarh	15.9
18.	Northern Hilly States	14.6
19.	Delhi	10.6
20.	Kerala	08.6
	All India	41.3

Note: Financial Exclusion I defined as non-access of financial instrument (books/postal savings insurance/MFS/Equities/chit funds/NBFCS/ Community based thrift)

Source: Invest India incomes and saving survey, 2007 E.T.P 15, 02.01.2011

Regulatory Challenges are to see the fallowings:

(*i*) viability

(*ii*) security

(*iii*) capacity

(*iv*) cash handling

(*v*) setting of local service points

(*vi*) enrolment process - time consuming and identity problems

(*vii*) issue of personalization cards

(*viii*) connectivity problems

(*ix*) reconciliation of transaction with BC and CBS

(*x*) bank staff not confidant at operating level

(*xi*) BC cum technology vendor is an ideal combination

(*xii*) prospective BCs are sitting on the fence and watching others.

Similarly the *Social challenges* are:

(*i*) rural populace having inhibition to approach bank branches

(*ii*) illiteracy of lower economy status so inhibition

(*iii*) lack of active customer education campaign.

Scheduled Commercial Bank Particulars

Indications	1969 (June)	1979	1989	1999 (March)	2006 (March	2007 (March)
Total Branches	8262	30202	57699	64939	69417	73836
Urban Branches	3108	9024	13519	17914	23271	26792
Rural Branches	5154	21178	44280	47025	46146	47044
Population per office (000)	64	21	14	15	16	-

Source: *Yojana*, Feb, 2010 issue p. 48.

N.B: It is seemed that the population per office was 13200 for March 2011.

Measures of RBI to include financial exclusions:

The measures are:

(*i*) Opening of "no frills" account with low or nil minimum balances as well as charges with regional languages.

(*ii*) Simplified procedure for KYC for customer of bank balances of Rs. 50000 and for credit of Rs. 1,00000.

(*iii*) Issue of a general credit card for Rs. 25,000.

(*iv*) Security purpose.

(*v*) Deregulated interest rate.

(*vi*) One time settlement of overdue loans up to Rs. 25,000 and again free access to credit.

Recent trends to improve financial inclusion: The following measures have been introduced to promote financial inclusion:

(*i*) Availability of "no frill" accounts

(*ii*) Simplifying KYC norms

(*iii*) Introducing of even credit cards in rural/semi-urban areas

(*iv*) Introduction of Business Facilitator (BF) and Business Correspondent (BC) model

(*v*) Setting the "Financial inclusion and FIT funds" with NABARD to provide funding support.

The finance ministry in the budget of 2007-08 has created funds for financial inclusion: the first is called Financial Inclusion Fund for developmental and promotional intervention and the other is Financial Inclusion Technology Fund to meet the cost of technology adoption of about $125 million each. The scope of using these funds are for the setting up of financial literacy centers and credit counseling on a pilot basis, launching a national financial literacy campaign, forging linkages with informal sources with suitable safeguards through appropriate legislation, evolving industry wise standards for IT solution, facilitating low cost remittance products are some of the initiative currently underway for furthering financial inclusion.

Conclusion

The financial system today encompasses a host of institutions including 75,170 branches of commercial, mainly public sector banks across the country; 15,612 branches of 82 regional rural banks; more than 14000 cooperative bank branches; 95,626 outlets of primary agricultural credit cooperative societies, NBFCS mutual fund companies and so on, yet the problem of exclusion from access to formal financial services is so acute that despite that penetrative outreach of the financial system 50 percent of the country is unbanked, (source: report on trend and progress of banking in India, 2010) with the access of banking services being limited in rural areas, the reliance on informal sources of finance is considerably high. The divide across various geographical regions too is significant in terms of access to banking services. The western, southern and northern regions have been far ahead of the northeastern, eastern and central regions not only in terms of branch intensity but also in terms of per capita deposit and credit. It is thus apparent that addressing financial exclusion will require a holistic approach in creating awareness about financial products, education and advice on money management, debt counseling, savings and affordable credit. Specific strategies to expand and outreach of their services have to be under taken in order to promote financial inclusion by expanding and promoting the available financial and banking infrastructures of the country.

REFERENCES

Cab calling Oct-Dec Issue, 2008, Reserve Bank of India, Mumbai

Dhara PK, *Indian Economy*, Ed. 2011

Economy survey of Odisha 2009-10, 2010-11, 2011-12, 2012-13 Publications of Planning and Co-ordination Department, Govt. of Odisha.

Samaja, Daily issue of August 12th, 2013 a publication of loka sevak mandala cuttack, Odisha

Yogakshema Oct-2007, issue. A publication of LIC of India

Yojana, Feb-2010 issue

Yojana, Jim-2011 issue

ANNEXURE

Population per commercial bank branch, March, 2011

Sl.No.	State	Population per Branch in thousand
1.	Bihar	25
2.	Nagaland	21
3.	Assam	21
4.	Uttar Pradesh	19
5.	Chhattisgarh	18
6.	West Bengal	17
7.	Madhya Pradesh	17
8.	Arunachal Pradesh	16
9.	Rajasthan	16
10.	Tripura	15
11.	Meghalaya	14
12.	Odisha	14
13.	Maharashtra	13
14.	Gujarat	12
15.	Jammu and Kashmir	12
16.	Andhra Pradesh	11
17.	Tamil Nadu	11
18.	Mizoram	11
19.	Karnataka	10
20.	Haryana	10
21.	Kerala	7
22.	Delhi	7
23.	Punjab	7
24.	Sikkim	7
25.	Himachal Pradesh	6
26.	Goa	3

Source: Economic Survey of Odisha, 2011-2012, p.182 planning and coordination department. Govt. of Odisha Distribution of branches in rural, semi urban and urban Areas, 2010-11.

14

Management of NPAs of Nationalized Banks of India

—G. Chandrayya*

Introduction

A well-built banking sector is important for developing economy. Indian banking system plays a vital role in the development of Indian economy. The primary function of the banking system is to mobilize the savings of the people by accepting different types of deposits from the public. In order to assemble deposits, banks undertake deposit mobilization through various deposit schemes suited to the different sections of the people. The banking industry has undergone a sea change after the first phase of economic liberalization in 1991 and hence credit management. While the primary function of banks is to lend money as loans and advances to various sectors such as agriculture, industry, personal loans, housing loans etc., but in recent times the banks have become very cautious in extending loans because of the mounting of NPAs. Non-Performing Assets (NPAs) reflect the performance of banks. The NPAs growth involve the necessity of provisions, which reduces the overall profits and shareholders' value.

Evolution and Growth of Banking in India

The History of Banking begins with the first prototype banks of merchants in the ancient world, which made grain loans

*Lecturer in Commerce, Government College (Autonomous), Rajahmundry, East Godavari.

to farmers and traders who carried goods between cities. This began around 2000 BC in Assyria and Babylonia.

In ancient India there is evidence of loans from the Vedic period (beginning 1750 BC). Later during the Maurya dynasty (321 to 185 BC), an instrument called *adesha* was in use, which was an order on a banker desiring him to pay the money of the note to a third person, which corresponds to the definition of a bill of exchange as we understand it today.

The existence of professional banking in India could be traced to the 500 BC. Kautilya's *Arthashastra,* dating back to 400 BC contained references to creditors, lenders and lending rates. Banking was fairly varied and catered to the credit needs of the trade, commerce, agriculture as well as individuals in the economy. The first bank of a joint stock variety was Bank of Bombay, established in 1720 in Bombay.

Definition of Bank

Banking Regulation Act, 1949, Section 5(c), defines bank as "a banking company which transacts the business of banking in India." Further, Section 5(b) of the BR Act defines banking as, 'accepting, for the purpose of lending or investment, of deposits of money from the public, repayable on demand or otherwise and withdrawable, by cheque, draft, and order or otherwise.'

Nationalization of Banks

The need for nationalization was felt because government believed that private commercial banks were lacking in fulfilling the social and developmental goals of banking. Nationalized banks in India are the major players in Indian banking system dominating the industry. Not only that, the Indian Nationalized Banks also play pivotal role in the economic development of the country at the same time.

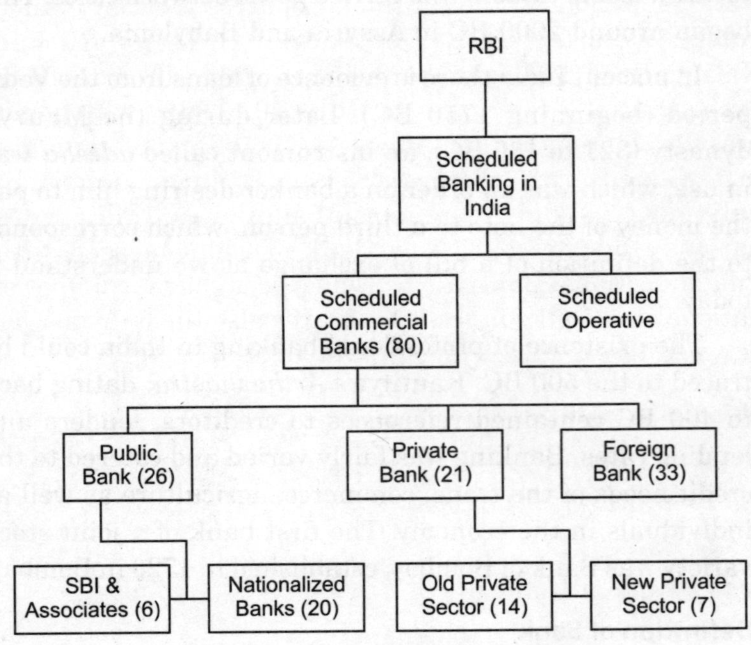

Fig. 14.1 : Banking Structure in India

The Base

The history of nationalization of Indian Banks dates back to the year 1955 when the Imperial Bank of India was Nationalized and re-named as State Bank of India (under the SBI Act, 1955). Later on July 19, 1960, the 7 subsidiaries of State Bank of India were also nationalized with deposits more than 200 crores.

The Initiative

The banking industry in India became a major tool for the development of country's economy by the 1960. This industry also became a large employer creating a number of opportunities for the job-seekers. In order to spread banking infrastructure in rural areas, the then Prime Minister, Indira Gandhi took the initiative to nationalize some commercial banks. She submitted a paper "Stray thoughts on Bank

Nationalization" in the All India Congress Meeting, which got positive feedback. The Indian Government had Nationalized 14 major banks with individual deposits exceeding Rs. 50 crore on July 19, 1969, which got presidential approval on August 9, 1969. In 1980, in order to provide government more power and command over credit delivery, six more commercial banks in India were nationalized. In 1993, New Bank of India merged with Punjab National Bank (PNB), which brought the number of nationalized banks in India to 19. It's also the only merger between two Indian nationalized banks.

List of Nationalized Banks in India

(1) Allahabad Bank,
(2) Andhra Bank,
(3) Bank of Baroda,
(4) Bank of India,
(5) Bank of Maharashtra,
(6) Canara Bank,
(7) Central Bank of India,
(8) Corporation Bank,
(9) Dena Bank,
(10) Indian Bank,
(11) Indian Overseas Bank,
(12) Oriental Bank of Commerce,
(13) Punjab & Sind Bant,
(14) Punjab National Bank,
(15) Syndicate Bank,
(16) UCO Bank,
(17) Union Bank of India,
(18) United Bank of India,
(19) Vijaya Bank.

The Concept of NPAs

The Non-Performing Asset (NPA) concept is limited to loans, advances and investments. As long as an asset generates the income expected from it and does not disclose any unusual risk other than normal commercial risk, it is treated as Performing Asset, and when it fails to generate the expected income it becomes a "Non-Performing Asset". In other words, a loan asset becomes a NPA when it stops to generate income, i.e., interest, fees, commission or any other dues for the bank for more than 90 days.

Meaning of Non-Performing Assets

Non-performing Assets (NPAs) are the smoking gun threatening the very stability of Indian banks. NPAs spoil a bank's profitability both through a loss of interest income and write-off of the principal loan amount itself. Banks assets are of various types. All those assets which generate periodical income are called as Performing Assets (PA). While all those assets which do not generate periodical income are called as Non-Performing Assets.

If the customers do not repay principal amount and interest for a certain period of time then such loans become NPA. In India, the time frame given for classifying the asset as NPA is 180 days as compared to 45 days to 90 days of international norms.

Definition of NPA

According to RB1, an asset, including a leased asset, becomes Non-Performing when it ceases to generate income for the bank. Non-Performing asset means an asset or account of borrower, which has been classified by bank as sub-standard, doubtful or loss asset, in accordance with the direction or guidelines relating to assets classification issued by RBI. A. non-performing asset is a loan or an advance where:

- Interest and/ or instalment of principal remain overdue for a period of more than 90 days in respect of a Term Loan (TLs),

- The account remains 'out of order' in respect of an Overdraft/Cash Credit (ODs/CCs),
- The bill remains overdue for a period of more than 90 days in the case of Bills Purchased (BPs)/Bills Discounted (BDs),
- A loan granted for short duration crops will be treated as NPA, if the installment of principal or interest thereon remains overdue for two crop seasons,
- A loan granted for long duration crops will be treated as NPA, if the installment of principal or interest thereon remains overdue for one crop season.

Types of NPAs

- *Gross NPA*

Gross NPA reflects the quality of the loans made by banks. It consists of all the non-standard assets like as sub-standard, doubtful, and loss assets. Gross NPAs Ratio can be calculated with the help of following formula:

Gross NPAs Ratio = Gross NPAs / Gross Advances

- *Net NPA*

Net NPA are those type of NPAs in which the bank has deducted the provision regarding NPAs. Net NPA shows tbe actual burden of banks. It can be calculated by the following formula:

Net NPAs = Gross NPAs – Provisions / Gross Advances - Provisions.

- **Sub-standard :** The account-holder belonging to this category don't pay three instalment continuously after 90 days and up to one year. Bank has made 10% provision of funds for this category to meet the losses generated from NPA from their profit.
- **Doubtful NPA :** Doubtful NPA are classified into three sub categories :
- 20% provision is made by the banks for D1 i.e. up to 1 year

- 30% provision is made by the bank for D2 i.e. up to 2 year
- 100% provision is made by the bank for D3 i.e. up to 3 year.

Loss Assets : When account holder belongs to this category 100% provision is made by the banks to write off their accounts. After this the assets are delivered to recovery agents for the purpose of sale.

Reasons behind NPA:

- Default of a loan intentionally
- Frequent shuffle of government policies leads to NPA.
- Customer has taken the loan for non-performance of business
- Most of the loan sanctioned for agricultural purposes
- Negligent pre-enquiry by the bank for sanctioning the loan to a customer.

Effects of NPA on Banks and FI

- Continuous draining of profit.
- Negative impact on goodwill.
- Adverse growth of equity value.
- Restricted cash flow by bank due to provision of fund created against NPA.

Methodology

Statement of Problem

Non-Performing Assets of banks are one of the biggest obstacles in the way of socio-economic development of India. The level of NPAs of the banking system in India is still too high. It affects the financial standing of the banks so that it is a heavy burden to the banks.

The problem of NPAs is not limit to only Indian public sector banks, but it prevails in the entire banking industry. Major portion of bad debts in Indian Banks arose out of lending to the priority sector at the commands of politicians and bureaucrats. To improve recovery and to minimize NPAs, banks are expected to do a continuous recovery exercise through various methods adopting newer strategies. Besides, the borrowers are to be educated again and again about the benefits they come from bank loans comparing to the local money lenders. This study was undertaken to analyze the management, to find the trend and assess the comparative position of NPAs in Nationalized Banks in India.

Research Design

The research design used to carry out this study is analytical research because it deals with statistical data and the main aim of the report is to analyze the factors affecting the problem mentioned. The present study is an analytical study, for this study secondary data are collected from the annual reports of Indian Nationalized Banks, Reserve Bank of India's website and other published information in various journals and magazines,

Sources of Data

The data collected is mainly secondary in nature. The sources of data for this study include the literature published by Nationalized Banks, the Reserve Bank of India and various magazines and journals dealing with the current banking scenario.

Objectives of the Study

The objectives of the present study are:

- Highlight the NPAs position of All Nationalized Banks in India
- To find the trend in NPAs of the above-mentioned banks
- Assess the comparative position of NPAs in Nationalized Banks.

Analysis of Data

The study is analytical in nature, and it is based on the secondary data. This study analyses the growth, trend and management of NPAs of Nationalized Banks. The scope of the study is limited to the analysis of NPAs of all the Nationalized Banks over the period of 2008-2012. It examines trend of Gross NPAs, Net NPAs; and assess the quality of NPA management and rank them as per mean of last five years. The data have been analyzed using percentage method, and selected statistical tools such as descriptive statistics, compound annual growth rate and one-way ANOVA (Analysis of Variance).

Table 14.1 : Analysis Gross Non-performing Assets and Descriptive Statistics and Ranks of Individual Banks

BANK	YEAR								
	2008	2009	2010	2011	2012	MEAN	SD	CAGR	RANK
Allahabad Bank	2	1.81	1.69	1.8	1.91	1.84	0.12	-0.89	7
Andhra Bank	1.1	0.83	0.86	1.38	2.12	1.26	0.53	14.06	4
Bank of Baroda	1.8	1.27	1.42	1.62	1.89	1,6	0.26	0.97	6
Bank of India	1.7	1.71	2.86	2.64	2.91	2.36	0.61	11.31	12
Bank of Maharashtra	2.6	2.29	2.96	2.47	2.28	2.52	0.28	2.62	15
Canara Bank	1.3	1.56	1.53	1.47	1.75	1.52	0.16	6.11	5
Central Bank of India	3.2	2.67	2.32	1.82	4.83	2.97	1.16	8.57	19
Corporation Bank	1.5	1.14	1.02	0.91	1.26	1.17	0.23	-3.37	2
Dena Bank	2.4	2.13	1.8	1.86	1.67	1.97	0.29	-6.96	8
Indian Bank	1.2	0.89	0.88	0.99	1.94	1.18	0.44	10.05	3
Indian Overseas Bank	1.6	2.54	4.47	2.71	2.79	2.82	1.04	11.75	16
Oriental Bank of Commerce	2.3	1.53	1.74	1.98	3.17	2.14	0.64	6.61	9
Punjab & Sind Bank	0.7	0.65	0.72	0.99	1.65	0.94	0.42	18.65	1
Punjab National Bank	2.7	1.77	1.81	1.79	3.15	2.24	0.64	3.11	10
Syndicate Bank	2.7	1.93	2.19	2.65	2.75	2.44	0.36	0.36	14
UCO Bank	3	2.21	1.99	3.31	3.73	2.85	0.73	4.44	17
Union Bank of India	2.2	1.96	2.29	2.37	3.16	2.4	0.45	7.48	13
United Bank of India	2.7	2.85	3.21	2.51	3.41	2.94	0.37	4.76	18
Vijaya Bank	1.6	1.95	2.37	2.56	2.93	2.28	0.52	12.86	11

Source: RBI.

Table 14.1 shows the gross NPA ratio of Nationalized Banks for last five years with necessary statistics like mean, growth rate of NPAs via CAGR (Compound Annual Growth Rate). From the above table it is seen that gross NPA of Nationalized Banks is in the upward trend generally in all the banks with varying growth. The CARG of banks under study is in the range of 6.96 to 14.06 and banks are having value of compound annual growth rate of gross NPAs during this range. As per the-mean which is representative of a group of data, banks are ranked in ascending order.

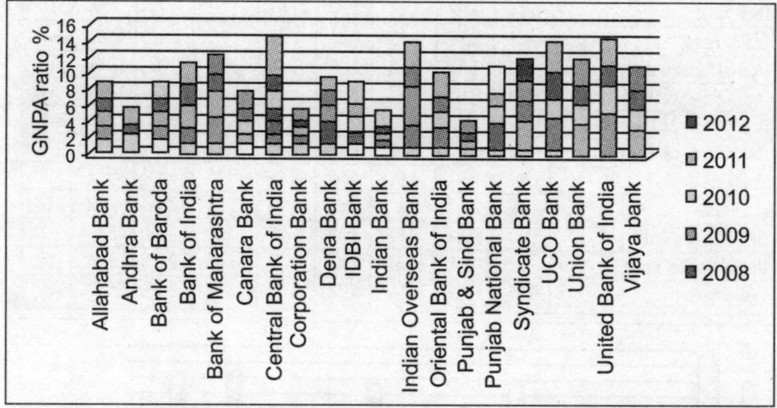

Fig. 14.2 : The above diagram interprets the GNPA ratio of all the banks for a five-year period and break of individual bar shows the annual gross NPA ratios for a five year period. From the figure it is shows that Punjab and Sind Bank (P&SB), Indian Bank, Corporation Bank and Andhra Bank have kept strict control on their NPAs

Table 14.2 displays the net non-performing assets ratio of Nationalized Banks. From the analysis of above table it is concluded that net NPA of Nationalized Banks is close alertness and control in most of the banks by maintaining sufficient level and of provisions to counter balance the decrease in the quality of assets. The ranking of banks is done on the basis of mean for last five years, and ranking is done in ascending order i.e. lower the average better the rank, Andhra Bank, Bank of Maharashtra, Corporation got first second and third rank respectively.

Table 14.2: Net Non-performing Assets and Descriptive Statistics and Ranks of Individual Banks

BANK	YEAR								
	2008	2009	2010	2011	2012	MEAN	SD	CAGR	RANK
Allahabad Bank	0.8	0.72	0.66	0.79	0.98	0.79	0.12	4.14	7
Andhra Bank	0.15	0.18	0.17	0.38	0.91	0.36	0.32	43.41	1
Bank of Baroda	0.47	0.31	0.34	0.35	0.54	0.4	0.1	2.82	2
Bank of India	0.52	0.44	1.31	0.91	1.47	0.93	0.46	23,1	9
Bank of Maharashtra	0.87	0.79	1.64	1.32	0.84	1.09	037	-0.7	11
Canara Bank	6~84	1.09	1.06	1.11	1.46	1.11	0.22	11.69	13
Central Bank of India	1.45	1.24	0.69	0.65	3.09	1.42	0.99	16.34	17
Corporation Bank	0.32	0.29	0.31	0.46	0.87	0.45	0.24	22.14	3
Dena Bank	0.94	1.09	1.21	1.22	1.01	1.09	0.12	1.45	11
Irfdian Bank	0.24	0.18	0.23	0.53	1.33	0.5	0.48	40.84	4
Indian Overseas Bank	0.6	1.33	2.52	1.19	1.35	1.4	0.7	17.61	16
Oriental Bank of Commerce	0.99	0.65	0.87	0.98	2.21	1.14	0.61	17.42	14
Punjab & Sind Bank	0.37	0.32	0.36	0.56	1.19	0.56	0.36	26.32	5
Punjab National Bank	0.64	0.17	0.53	0.85	1.52	0.74	0.5	18.89	6
Syndicate Bank	0.97	0.77	1.07	0.97	0.96	0.95	0.11	-0.21	10
UCO Bank	1.98	1.18	1.17	1.84	1.96	1.63	0.42	-0.2	19
Union Bank of India	0.17	0.34	0.81	1.19	1.7	0.84	0.62	58.49	8
United Bank of India	1.1	1.48	1.84	1.42	1.72	1.51	0.29	9.35	18
Vijaya Bank	0.57	0.82	1.4	1.52	1.72	1.21	0.49	24.72	15

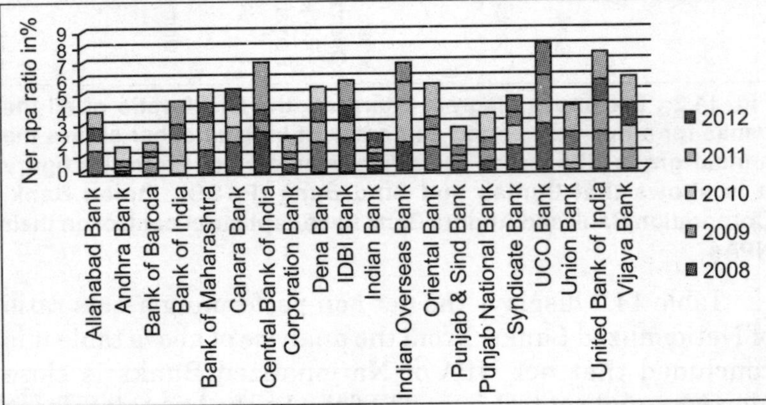

Fig. 14.3 : The above bar chart shows the annual ratios of net NPAs for five year term for each Nationalized Bank and height of bars determine level of NNPAs and division of bars determine annual level of annual NPPA ratio. Andhra Bank, Bank of Baroda, Corporation bank, Indian Bank and Punjab and Sind Bank are positive in terms of NNPA ratio as there level is minimum and rest having higher ratio with varying level of bars and UCO Bank displayed bar length is maximum.

Table 14.3

BANK	ITEM			
	Rank as per GNPAS	Rank asper NNPA	Average	Overall Rank
Allahabad Bank	7	7	7	6
Andhra Bank	4	1	2.5	1.5
Bank of Barpda	6	2	4	5
Bank of India	13	9	11	10.5
Bank of Maharashtra	16	11	13.5	14
Canara Bank	5	13	9	8
Central Bank of India	20	18	19	18
Corporation Bank	21	3	2.5	1.5
Dena Bank	9	11	10	9
Indian Bank	3	4	3.5	4
Indian Overseas Bank	17	17	17	16
Oriental Bank of Commerce	10	14	12	12
Punjab & Sind Bank	1	5	3	3
Punjab National Bank	11	6	8.5	7
Syndicate Bank	15	10	12.5	13
UCO Bank	18	20	19	18
Union Bank of India	14	8	11	10.5
United Bank of India	19	19	19	18
Vijaya Bank	12	16	14	15

Table 14.3 shows the composite rank of each bank, this is arrived at by averaging the ranks of bank as per GNPA and NNPA. So final ranks assigned to banks is based on the average of earlier tw ranks. It can be seen from the table that Andhra Bank and Corporation Bank has got first ran followed by Punjab and Sind Bank at second rank and Indian Bank at third rank.

Table 14.4

GNPA	Sum of Squares	DF	Mean Square	F	Table value at 5 level of Sig. F(19,80)
Between	37.595	19	1.979	6.516	1.718
Within	24.295	80	0.304		
Total	61.89	99			

Table 14.4 shows that calculated F value of 6.516 is which is very much higher than table value or critical value of 1.718 at 5% level of significance with degrees of freedom (v_1 = 19 and v_2 = 80) and hence our analysis supports our hypothesis that there is significant difference of gross NPA ratios of nationalized banks. This shows that nationalized banks are having different level of gross NPAs and which shows their efficiency in management of gross NPAs, and quality of their assets.

Table 14.5
ANOVA

GNPA	Sum of Squares	DF	Mean Square	F	Table value at 5 level of Sig. F(19,80)
Between	13.753	19	0.724	3.583	1.718
Within	16.163	80	202		
Total	29.915	99			

Table 14.5 shows the ANOVA test of Net NPA to Net Advances of Nationalized banks. It is seen from the table that calculated F statistics value of 3.583 is higher than table value of 1.718 at 5% level of significance. Results of our ANOVA analysis support our hypothesis that there is significant difference between NNPA of Nationalized banks, which shows their varied performance of asset management.

Conclusion

From the study it is quite evident that the NPAs have a negative influence on the achievement of capital adequacy level, funds mobilization and deployment policy, banking system credibility, productivity and overall economy. The management of NPAs is a discouraging task for every bank in the banking industry. The very important reason and necessity for management of NPA is due to their multi-dimensional effect on the operations, performance and position of bank. It is found that level of NPA both gross and net is on an average in upward trend all the nationalized banks but the growth rate is different. Banks got different ranks on the basis of mean and final ranking was done on the basis of average gross NPA rank and net NPA rank.

Recommendations

- Banks should find out the original reasons/purposes of the loan required by the borrower.
- Framing reasonably well documented loan policy and rules.
- Sound credit appraisal on well-settled banking norms with emphasis on reduction in Gross NPAs rather than Net NPAs
- Position of overdue accounts is reviewed on a weekly basis to arrest slippage of fresh account to NPA.
- Based on the recent trends, banks should emphasize more on priority sector for reducing the quantum of NPAs.
- Banks should ensure that there is no diversion of funds disbursed to the borrower.
- Bank officials should frequently visit the unit and should assess, the physical conditions of the assets, receivables and stocks therein.

REFERENCES

Aryasri, & Murthy: *Banking: Banking & Financial Systems*, Tata McGraw-Hill, 2003.

Berger A. and De Young R. (1997) *Journal of Banking & Finance*, Vol. 21.

Bidam, S.N. (2002) *Managing Non-Performing Assets in Banks*, Vision Books, New Delhi.

Journals issued by The Institute of Chartered Accountants of India (ICAI). *Journal of Information and Operations Management.*

Shivepuje, C.R., Kaveri V.S. (1997) *Management of Non-Performing Advances*, Sultan Chand & Sons, New Delhi.

The Economics Times.

vww.businessstandard.com.

www.economictimes.com.

www.rbi.org.in.

www.wikipedia.org

Index